A Journey Through Life

FRED S. HIRSEKORN

To Dr. Bob — on his 66th

For your care and what you
have done for so many others

Fred S. Hirsek

Produced by:

FriesenPress

Suite 300 – 852 Fort Street
Victoria, BC, Canada V8W 1H8

www.friesenpress.com

Distributed to the trade by The Ingram Book Company

TABLE OF CONTENTS

I   Preface

II   Acknowledgements

III   Dedication

v   In Memory of Robin

1   THE YOUNG YEARS

2   Parody on Multiple Nursery Rhymes

4   Parody on Nursery Rhymes 2

5   Afraid to Fly.

7   The Dragon

9   My Life Reads Like Fiction

12   It Made My Day

15   The Monster

17   The Professional

18   Chocolate Pudding

21   Letter to Grandparents from Eagle River, Michigan

24   The heart of a 10 year old

28   We are Moving Where?

31   The Rusty Weather Vane

34   A Boring Vacation

35   The Explorer

39   THE MIDDLE YEARS

     40   It All Started With a Kiss
     41   Dancing
     43   She Opened the Door
     45   The Good News
     47   Culture Shock
     49   Changes and Shifts in a lifetime
     51   The Voice Inside My Head
     52   Down and Out?
     54   Fighting the Squirrels
     56   The Limits of Passion
     58   My Magic Piano
     59   Just for Today
     61   Mental Clutter
     64   Perplexed and Regrets
            A difficult Relationship
     68   Forgiveness
     70   The Rose
     71   Yesterday, Today, Tomorrow
     73   What was I Thinking?

77   THE (G)OLDEN YEARS

     78   Rejuvenation
     79   At This Stage of the Journey
     82   It's Never too Late
     84   A Hole in One
     86   Ode to Susan on her 60th Birthday
     88   Feeling Old
     90   Getting Old
     92   It Takes a Little Oil
     93   A Curve in the Road
     95   Motivation
     98   What is Most Important?

100 Ode To my Beloved wife
     on Our 63rd Anniversary
101 An Old Spouse's Love
103 Old but the Flame Still Glows
104 Real Love
105 What is Passion?
106 What is Love?
108 Quiet Chaos
110 Who am I?
112 Memories
114 In My World
116 A Variable Season
117 How do People See Me?
119 Stressful Suspension
122 Roles I've have played
124 Special Meaning
126 The Inanimate Walls
127 The Mother-in-Law
129 The Old Grouch
131 The Perfect Day
133 The Reunion
134 From a Withered Tree a Flower Blooms
136 A Treasured Tree has Fallen
138 Closure
141 A Box of Tears
143 I Feel No Fear
145 We Come, We Experience, We Leave
146 The Four Seasons

149 GERMANY
150 The Early Years
153 The Gathering Storm
157 The Survivors Miracles
160 Everyone Will Understand You

163   W W I I

    164 Getting into the War
    166 Early Training
    168 The Idiots Won the War
    170 Heading Overseas – Discordant
    172 First Combat
    174 Two Impulsive Acts
    176 A Quick Decision
    179 A Loveable Rascal
    180 A Close Encounter
    181 The Futility of War
    186 Unsung Heroes

189   C R E A T I V E W R I T I N G

    190 On being Creative
    192 The Early Writing Obstacle
    194 Landing Words on Paper
    195 Why Do I Write?
    197 A Wonderful Escape
    199 The Rhythm
    201 A written Pilgrimage
    203 Don Quixote
    205 An Adapted Poem
    207 In Search for an Oasis
    209 Her Trembling Lips
    210 Ruby Red Lips
    211 Jump off and fly?
    213 A Confusing Language
    215 The Use of Words
    217 Lost and Obsolete Words
    219 Obsolete but not Forgotten
    221 Paraprosdokians
    222 Savor the Moments
    223 The Musical Tree

224   The Sound of Silence

226   Pearls Upon a Page

228   The Pencils Job

229   The Treasure Hunt

231   The Wise Person Within

232   Why Do I Care

234   TV ads

235   Writing a Creative Epic

237   Words Scrambled in My Head

239   THOUGHT PROVOKING

240   Admirable Qualities

242   Finding Serenity

244   My Search for GOD

248   Our Choice

250   Quiet Dignity

253   Serendipity

255   I'll Just Be Me

256   Sometimes I Wonder

258   What is the 'IT?'

261   Two Crows

263   About the Author

Preface

The rainbow is a metaphor of our path through life. We slowly reach the peak of performance. A slow decline follows. We have a multitude of experiences both on the way up and on the way down; some are like the brighter colors of the rainbow, some are like the darker ones. Most experiences add to our wisdom.

I was born in Germany in 1924. My journey through life has had many sharp turns; some to the brighter side, some to the darker side. In retrospect the darker turns had some brightness and the brighter ones some darkness.

I started writing my autobiography *The Winds of Change* after retiring in 1994. After many years of research and writing I experienced writer's block. A search for a breakthrough in 2008 led me to a creative writing class taught by Peter Blau, a Minneapolis Loft instructor. He added a bright color to my rainbow. The focus of the class, creativity, discovered a new, challenging, and exciting freedom of expression (and sense of humor) within me.

The short stories and poems selected for this book are among the many written over the last six years. Some are fact and some are fiction. Some are humorous, some are serious, some are thought provoking, and some are simply meant to entertain. Some can help open communications between parents and children. The stories are bundled into the stages of our lives, from early age to middle age and to old age with some significant experiences encountered during the journey. Each story and poem however is self standing.

Acknowledgements

My gratitude to Brelan Boyce, Author Account Manager at Friesen Press, who patiently guided me through the publication process. Thanks also to Peter Blau who spent much time proof reading the manuscript. There are actions which touch the heart and continue to resonate long thereafter. Eventually they rise to a crescendo which exceeds the ability to articulate their impact. Our daughter Susan Ahlquist has been interested in my writings from the time I attended the creative writing class six years ago. Her interest and support throughout this venture has added motivation which significantly enhanced the pleasure of my writing and enabled publishing these poems and short stories. I am ever grateful to my wife, Barbara who, since our marriage in 1948, has added a most brilliant color to my rainbow.

It is my hope that the reader will enjoy *A Journey Through Life* as much as I enjoyed writing it. I hope it will evoke many memories of your own.

Dedication

This book is dedicated in memory of our daughter, Robin Greenwood. She did not survive breast cancer and passed away in 1991. She left three young children, Heather, Eleni, and Seth. She would have been very proud to see the exceptional adults they have become. A percentage of the income from the sale of this book will go to further breast cancer research.

In Memory of Robin

1956–1991

We drive down life's road
And admire the scene
When lo and behold
There's a sight never seen.

Like a diamond
With many beautiful facets
It leaves a warm glow
Then too rapidly passes.

Yet it leaves behind
Etched deep in our hearts
Three new vistas
Which that sight imparts.

Each one sparkles and recalls
That touching new wonderful sight
Whose quality was felt by us all
Then faded gently into the night.

And so to the beauty
Which too early was banished
She will never be forgotten
Although the sight has vanished.

THE YOUNG YEARS

Parody on Multiple Nursery Rhymes

Humpty Dumpty went to the Mall
Humpty Dumpty had a great ball.
All of his credit was well overspent
So he lost his home which was not his intent.

Baa, baa black sheep,
Have you any cash,
No sir, no sir,
Can't pay for Humpty's bash.

Twinkle twinkle little star,
Let old Humpty sell his car,
Let him use the money supply
And learn to save and not to buy.

A tisket, a tasket
And afore you asket,
None would lend Humpty any cash
So Humpty looked for a place to crash.

Three blind mice, three blind mice.
See they run. See how they run.
They all ran toward a hole in the wall
Into which they all could safely crawl,
Chased by a cat wanting to eat them all
Three blind mice.

Once safely inside, guess what they found
Sitting on the sofa just playing around
It was Humpty Dumpty all out of dough
To him this was a good place to lie low.
With the three blind mice.

Parody on Nursery Rhymes 2

Jack and Jill went up the hill
To smoke some marijuana
Jack got high and began to fly
And was last seen over Botswana

Jack and Jill rode to a pub
To celebrate their marriage
They brought their pail
To be filled with ale
Aboard a horse drawn carriage.

Hey diddle diddle
Nero played his fiddle
While Rome continued to burn.
He needed the heat to roast his meat
And to dine with the wine from his urn.

Afraid to Fly.

Once upon a time a family of robins lived in a big oak tree. There was a little robin named Robert. Robert robin was very small for his age. All of his brothers and sisters flew around and played all day, but poor Robert just sat in the tree and watched. It wasn't that he couldn't fly. Robert knew how to fly but was afraid to try it. His older siblings made fun of him and told him that he was so small that he would fall if he tried. His parents even scolded him for not keeping up with the others. He lost all confidence. It made him afraid to fly.

This went on for a long time until something happened that made Robert not afraid any more. This fear did not leave Robert all at once. It was deep seated due to his earlier experience. His father had often chastised Robert for being so weak and small. His father was a strong flyer. He bragged that he would fly one mile into strong head winds each day, just to demonstrate his prowess.

Why couldn't he be just as strong as his cousin Jeeps who hatched in the same tree shortly before Robert? After all, Robert had played with Jeeps and Jeeps liked him as well. Other larger and stronger of Robert's peers, including his own brothers and sisters, would often pick on Robert because he was so small and so different.

Robert eventually became afraid of high places. His father and mother were so busy feeding their second clutch of hungry fledglings 100 meals of worms and cutworms a day that they did not see Robert's growing fear.

Desperate for help Robert, who was very smart, sought the wisdom of an old owl that lived in the tree. He knew that owls are robins' predators, but he believed that they feed on the eggs, not on birds. The kind old owl took a liking to Robert and let him stay in his nest over the cold winter while all other robins, including Jeeps migrated to warmer climates. Robert really missed Jeeps, his only friend and playmate. He was sad that he would probably never see Jeeps again. The owl provided friendship and wisdom but Robert's fear persisted.

One spring Robert strolled to a close branch of the big oak tree and much to his delight spotted Jeeps who had migrated back to the old nesting place. They joyfully flapped their wings; their happy chirping was heard far beyond the tree.

Robert felt secure in the presence of Jeeps who appeared poised, self confident and who was truly happy to see him again.

Jeeps respected and admired all Robert had accomplished, lauded his strengths and was never judgmental. Robert was humbled by the love and respect his erudite cousin Jeeps had for him.

One day Jeeps asked Robert to fly with him to search for worms for his new clutch of fledglings. The fear of heights however still made Robert apprehensive.

"Come fly with me," said Jeeps. "We won't fly far and I will fly along side of you all the way. You are born to fly and you will be a good flier, as good as your dad." These encouraging words from his trusted friend made Robert want to try. Eventually Robert flew farther and farther, first with Jeeps, then alone. Robert began to enjoy helping gather worms for Jeep's kids.

It was a joyous occasion indeed when he was able to migrate south to warmer climates together with the entire Jeeps family the following fall. It was not easy for Robert to say goodbye to the kind and wise old owl. He promised to return the following spring.

The Dragon

Once upon a time there was boy named Donovan. Donovan was five years old. His favorite toy was a kite. He especially loved his grandfather, whom he called Saba. He got to spend some time with him whenever he visited Minnesota.

One day Saba said to Donovan "Let's go fly your kite. The wind is just right and I know a field where there are no wires in the way." Donovan ran to get his kite.

It was a sunny day. Puffy clouds slowly floated across the blue sky. Donovan let his kite fly higher and higher, the tail of the kite wagging happily in the breeze.

"Look, Saba, there is a cloud which looks like a dragon" shouted Donovan after a while. Sure enough one could see what looked like the claws and the face of the dragon. When the sun peeked out from the front of the face it looked like the dragon was spewing fire!

Donovan was so scared that he let loose the string to the kite. "Saba, Saba" he cried as the kite disappeared into the 'dragon'. "The dragon ate my kite." Very slowly the dragon cloud drifted away with the kite and Donovan cried.

Saba put his arm around Donovan and said, "You love to ride your bicycle. Let's go get our bicycles and follow the dragon. Together they rode along the dirt road following the lazily drifting dragon.

Donovan was very sad. Suddenly he spotted his kite at the side of the road. He could not believe it. He was so happy. He looked for the dragon in the sky and thought that he saw it wave good bye to him then slowly turn into a heart. It was only a cloud, but to Donovan it was a playful and friendly dragon.

My Life Reads Like Fiction

Danny age 6, loved to hear stories his grandfather Herman told. He had just heard his story about the little Robin who was afraid to fly. "Grandpa," he said, "tell me another story." "OK," Grandpa replied and Danny snuggled back into his arms.

"Once upon a time there was a little boy named Ernest who was born in a country far away. He loved to play soccer and he had many friends. They all called him Ernie. Soon however a very bad man became the leader of the country. He hated all people who believed in this little boy's religion. He got a lot of bad guys to break into the homes of these people and beat them up." "Grandpa," Danny interrupted, "couldn't they just call the police?" he asked.

"Danny, the police were afraid of these bad guys. There were so many of them that they would beat up on anyone who would try to interfere with them," Grandpa answered, "including the police."

"That's scary, Grandpa."

"Soon none of Ernie's friends would even speak to him and to the other kids who worshipped God the same way. Soon they too began to pick on Ernie. Then all children who worshipped God in the same way as Ernie did were no longer allowed to attend school." Grandpa continued. "So many scary things happened to Ernie and his parents that they had to flee this country and leave everything they had built for many generations. Even though they became very poor, they were lucky. They were among the few who were allowed to enter this great country called the United States. It saved their lives.

Ernie could not speak English and all the kids in his class called him stupid and made fun of him because he could not answer the simplest questions, and he spoke funny. Ernie almost cried he felt so alone and hurt."

"Grandpa, there is a kid in our class who is so slow and dumb that we all make fun of him," Danny quipped.

"Do you know just how hurt Ernie was and how hurt this kid in your class must be?" asked Grandpa. "Some kids are born with a learning disability and cannot help it." "Gee, I never thought about that. I feel bad about making fun of him now," Danny said remorsefully.

"Then you can try to become his friend and convince the other kids in your class to stop harassing him also." added Grandpa.

" Well, Ernie became a Boy Scout, and in a fun way learned a lot about how to take care of himself, to care for others, and to do his duty to God and our country. He quickly learned to speak English and rose to the rank of Eagle Scout. He played football in high school, worked hard and even made the National Honor Society." Grandpa continued.

"He was a soldier in World War II fighting the mean people who forced them to flee the country of his birth, rose to become first sergeant and was awarded two medals for heroism. Experiencing the horrors of war caused him to become him a very serious person. Many of the buddies around him did not survive the war."

"If war is so bad, Grandpa, why is there war?" asked Danny.

"Good question. It is because bad people, tyrants, want to rule the world and make us all live by their rules. They demand absolute obedience and loyalty only to themselves. They severely punish all who dare to even question them. People from freedom loving countries such as our United States try to talk to these tyrants. They never listen. So all free people eventually rise up to fight them. There eventually is no other way to stay free."

"Well, Ernie got married to a most wonderful girl. Thanks to our US Government, he was able to go to College and get a graduate degree," Grandpa continued. "This allowed him to get a good job. They had four children, all healthy and smart.

He was appointed to bigger and bigger jobs and eventually became a Vice President in a large company.

Along the way he saw many children, such as you have in your class, who were born with a learning disability. In his time they were taken away from their parents and kept locked up in institutions.

He was so grateful for having healthy children that he spent his spare time learning about this disability. Together with experts he found a way to teach them and to get jobs for them. This got thousands of these individuals out of the institutions. They enjoyed the work. They began to feel good about themselves. They performed much better than those without such disabilities.

Ernie's was very grateful to the Unites States for offering him all of these opportunities. He continued to do all he could to help improve the lives of as many people as possible in the various communities in which he and his family lived.

Ernie also got bigger and bigger jobs in various volunteer organizations. Now wasn't that a great fairy tale about little Ernie, Danny?" Grandpa asked.

"Grandpa, that is not a fairy tale," answered Danny.

"How do you know that it's not a fairy tale?" Grandpa said.

"Because Mommy told me some of these things have happened to you. I really tricked you, didn't I Grandpa?" Danny said as he climbed up to give Grandpa a hug.

"You sure did," replied Grandpa, "You sure did."

It Made My Day

The dishes are done; the laundry is done; the floors are swept; and the correspondence is in the mail. All is quiet in the house this afternoon. I sit at our kitchen table with a cup of coffee watching our seven-year-old son Johnny playing in the backyard. It is a beautiful summer day. My husband had built several birdhouses which he hung on branches of the tree near which Johnny was playing. A wet and warm spring had covered the tree with a full and splendid green coat. Puffs of gently floating white clouds backed by a perfectly blue sky further enhance the beauty of the tree.

Movement in the tree soon drew my attention. I could hear the song of the wrens, and the mourning doves. *They seem to be celebrating this moment also.*

I sat there engrossed by the beauty of the moment when suddenly the kitchen door burst open. Johnny comes rushing in all excited. "Mom, mom," he shouted. "I know what I want to be." This came as a complete surprise. When family or friends had asked him what he would like to be, he only shrugged his shoulders and, looking at the ground, he muttered a quiet "I don't know." Suddenly he seemed to have found exactly what he wants to be and was all excited about.

"My gosh, Johnny, tell me what it is you like to be."

"Mom, I want to be a bird."

"You would like to be…" I started to say but realized I had better think this answer through. I smiled as though I was happy that he found his future while my mind raced through the options.

I would crush his sudden enthusiasm by explaining the reality. I should really stop and think before answering.

"My goodness, Johnny, why do you want to be a bird?"

"I heard the birds singing happy tunes, and they protect our tree. It is so beautiful."

"How great it is that you want to protect our beautiful tree. I was looking out the kitchen window and was also admiring the tree. You have a great idea. You can help to expand it into the whole neighborhood," I responded, hoping that he would understand enough to listen further and with equal enthusiasm.

"I don't know how this could be as much fun as being a bird, Mom."

'Yes, the birds are a happy lot as long as the tree is healthy. When we don't have any rain for a long time the tree gets thirsty, its leaves dry out and the wind blows the dry leaves off the tree. The birds are very unhappy then. The hot winds blow them around and there is not enough food to feed their babies. Also when trees starve for water, insects are more likely to further damage them."

"Yeah, I remember when you and dad kept watering our tree. Is that why it look so much healthier than our neighbor's trees."

"Yes, Johnny. And that is why we have so many birds in our tree. Now, wouldn't it make you happy if you could help keep all of the trees in our neighborhood healthy with many birds singing in them?"

"But Mom, I can't go around watering all of the trees in our neighborhood."

"No, that's true. But when we have a dry spell, think about dropping a note in all of our neighbor's mail boxes asking them to please water their trees to keep them healthy. Maybe your whole class can take that on as a project which will not only keep the trees healthy but also make the birds happy. You will have done so much more than being one bird for a little while. Think about your having helped keeping many trees healthy with beautiful singing birds for everyone's pleasure. Wouldn't that really make you happy every time you walk down the street?

"I'll have to think about that, Mom."

Cleaning his room the next morning while he was away at school I found the first three copies of messages he had written to put into our neighbors mail boxes.

'Dear neighbor:' it read. 'Could you please water the trees in front of your house to keep them green and healthy when we don't have enough rain? I kinda like walking down our street when the trees are so beautiful. The birds like them also and they'll sing to you in the morning. I hope that you'll like it too. Thank you.

Your neighbor in the tan house,

Johnny'

It made my day.

The Monster

Lenny, age six, loved his grandfather. He felt safe and secure in his presence. After all, his 'grandpa' was a rough rider with Theodore Roosevelt who had captured San Juan Hill in Cuba in the war against the Spanish in 1898. Lenny always wanted to hear more of his war stories. He loved to ride into the countryside with his grandfather on his horse and wagon. His grandfather even allowed him to take the reins once as they trotted along the dirt roads.

One summer day grandpa had arranged to visit with some of his war buddies a few miles away and asked Lenny if he would like to ride along. The road took them through a forest laden with old and tall trees. Grandpa knew a lot about trees also. He pointed out the white pines which had grown over 80 feet tall, the majestic tall oak trees, and the shorter cone shaped linden trees as they travelled along the road.

It was obvious how much grandpa's friends admired him by their greetings. This pleased Lenny who became engrossed by the stories grandpa and his friends shared about their experiences during this war.

A loud thunderstorm delayed their return trip home until dark. When the storm passed, and the moon appeared in the clear night, they started their return home. Lenny had never driven through a dark forest but felt safe as he snuggled against his grandpa. The cool breeze, the rustling of the leaves and the steady rhythm of the horse's gait soon lulled Lenny asleep.

A sudden jolt woke Lenny. It was caused by the horse shying from a sight ahead and stopping. Lenny looked ahead and saw a frightening image and heard a scary sound. A huge fiery face glowed and faded and glowed over and over again at the side of the road about 30 yards ahead. The sound 'who, who,' accompanied the glow of the fiery face. "It's a monster Grandpa," Lenny shouted with fright. "I'm scared. Let's turn back."

Grandpa sat there silent for a moment pondering the situation. "Please grandpa, it will kill us. Please let's turn back NOW!"

"There are no monsters, Lenny" grandpa tried to reassure Lenny.

"Please, grandpa, please, I'm scared."

"We will drive closer and see what this monster really is, Lenny," Grandpa said.

Lenny, shivering with fright, held tight to his grandfather and closed his eyes as they approached the 'monster'.

"Open your eyes, Lenny, and look at your monster" came grandpa's calm voice.

Slowly Lenny turned his head from the protection of grandpa's arm and looked fearfully at the sight out of the corner of his eyes. There was the glowing ember of a tree which had been struck and set on fire by lightning. The gentle breeze made the embers glow brightly and wane when it subsided, over and over again.

"Lenny, there are explanations for all that we see. There are no monsters," his grandfather explained.

As they rode on they could still hear the owl ask "who, who," as though asking who had set the tree on fire.

The Professional

A few nights ago we played bridge with Chuck and Doris whose friendship we have enjoyed over the years. Their college grandson had just performed at a violin recital which drew standing applause.

"Did you know that Chuck was a professional violinist," asked Doris.

"No, we sure did not. We knew of his many talents and accomplishments but were not aware of his musical virtuosity. Perhaps that is the source of your grandson's talent," I responded.

"Well, not exactly, "she answered, "Can I tell them, Chuck?"

"Yah, go ahead, you've gone this far," he replied, his voice displaying a tinge of discomfort.

"Well, Chuck's mother loved violin music and insisted that he learns to play as he started high school. He became a professional quite early. The first payment Chuck received for his performance came from his father as Chuck practiced at home…... He paid him 25 cents to stop."

Chocolate Pudding

I held my mother's hand at the nursing home although I doubt that she knew who I was any more. Alzheimer disease had strengthened its hold over the last several years. Lean and frail, her hair had turned white and thin, she sits in her wheel chair dressed in her robe with her head down, her eyes closed.

I held back my tears as I recalled the very vital woman to whom I owe so much. How I wish I could have told her so while she could still understand. She raised us to live a well adjusted and good life. She taught us values. My mind wanders back many years when I was just nine years old. I loved her chocolate pudding, no other tasted so rich and creamy. She always had some in the refrigerator for me. So my gratification was always immediate.

"Mom, could I please have some chocolate pudding?" I asked.

"You like it so much that it's time to learn how to make it yourself," she replied.

Well, I thought, this ought to be a snap.

"Go to the cupboard and take out the cornstarch, sugar, salt, vanilla extract and the semisweet chocolate chips. Then get the milk from the refrigerator. You will also need to get the measuring cup, the measuring spoons, a scale, a whisk, a spatula, and a pot." she continued. I dutifully did as she asked but thought 'Oh my gosh, that is a load.'

"Now measure out and combine the cornstarch, sugar, and salt into the pot. Slowly whisk the milk into ingredients."

"Mom, a lot of the dry stuff is sticking to the bottom and sides of the pot," I said.

"That is why you need the spatula, honey. Scrape the bottom and sides of to make sure that all of the dry ingredients a mixed in. You don't like lumps in your pudding."

"OK, now what?"

"Turn the stove burners to a low flame and put the pot on the burner. You don't want the mixture to boil.

Stir it occasionally, scraping the bottom and sides of the pot, and use the whisk if lumps begin to form. You will add the chocolate when the mixture begins to thicken," she advised.

"Mom the stuff in the pot is bubbling."

"Turn down the flames until the bubbling stops."

"Mom, the mixture is not thickening."

"Keep stirring. I will take 15 to 20 minutes for it to thicken. Then add the chocolate and continue to stir until the pudding is smooth and thick."

This is work crept through my mind. But the taste of Mom's chocolate pudding made me continue. "The chocolate is in. Now what do I do?"

"Turn off the burners; take the pot off the stove; stir in the vanilla. Then pour the pudding onto serving dishes."

After I did, I asked, "Can I put some whipped cream on one of the puddings and have it now."

"No, honey, that will make if liquefy again. We have to let it cool down. I know that you don't like a skin on your pudding. To avoid that put plastic wrap on top of each pudding and smooth it down gently against the surface before you put the dishes into the refrigerator. Once cold it's your to enjoy. In the meanwhile you can help me clean up the pot and utensils."

"That's a lot of work and a long wait for just a few cups of pudding, Mom."

"Yes, honey, it is. The lesson to learn from this and to remember is that it takes a lot of planning and work to gain what you really want to achieve or enjoy. There is no such thing as having your needs and wishes achieved without it. There is no immediate gratification, a term you will hear often. Enjoy your pudding," she said and sat back.

What a teacher of life the wonderful woman whose hand I hold has been. How I wish I could have told her that and how I have tried to emulate her with my own children.

Letter to Grandparents from Eagle River, Michigan

May 1, 1881

Dear Grandpa and Grandma:

I am sorry I have not written for such a long time. I miss you very much. Moving here was the blackest day of my life. I miss my friends in Boston. There is nothing to do here. I just hate it. No candy store and no one to play with. Just a lot of water, trees, dirt roads and they say bears are around. There's just one store which sells everything but really doesn't. Why did papa have to take the lighthouse keeper's job in such a bad place? Mamma has to work so hard here.

We live in this house with the lighthouse. I miss my house in Boston. It was so much bigger and had much more room to play. I go to this little school with all these little kids. They are so dumb. Some speak German, Polish and some with a funny English. They say they came from Ireland. We are all in the same room. It has a painted blackboard and all we do is what they call diagramming sentences. I hate it. I don't like the teacher. There are no gas lights on the street at night like in Boston. It is so cold in the winter. There is so much snow we can't even get out. There is a stove in the school room. They burn logs in it but it really keeps only those sitting near it warm. I hate it.

September 22, 1881
Dear Grandpa and Grandma:

Papa just found the letter I started but somehow it got lost until just now. I did not finish it. So I'll do it now.

About a week ago some man came to our village. He must have been important because so many others came along. Many here went to see him. They said his name was James Garfield. You know what? Papa said that he was the president of the United States. The mailman who brings the mail to the general store with his horse and buggy said that President James Garfield was killed just a few days ago. That is how we learned who he was.

School is much better now. I have new friends in the village with whom I play. Most of the kids at school live too far away to go to see them. Most of their parents work in the copper mines. They came here from all over the world to find work there.

I learn so much at home. Papa took me up to where the lights are in the light house. Did you know that he lights the lights every night so the ships on Lake Superior don't lose their way? Papa says they burn sperm oil which comes from whales. Sometimes he lights the lights when there is fog or heavy snow. We use sperm oil in our lamps at home, sometimes even kerosene.

Mr. Garfield must have come here because it is really a fun place. Papa has taken me boating on the lake in our birch bark canoe. We have gone on hikes through the woods and saw many animal tracks. We saw deer and bears.

Those bear cubs are sure cute playing with each other. I bet you don't see those in Boston. We saw an eagle just yesterday. We can go fishing anytime. There's trout in the spring and salmon in the fall. I caught a big salmon a few days ago.

Papa chops wood and stores it for the winter. I love our fireplace. I even like the snow. I can curl up near the crackling fire in our fireplace and feel good and warm. The water splashing over the rocky shore line puts me asleep. When it looks like a snow storm is coming Mamma goes to the general store to stock up on stuff.

Do you know they even have green bananas there which last us for several days?

Everyone knows everyone in the village. They help each other out whenever it is needed. I sure like the people here. It's really a great place, Grandpa and Grandma. There are things here which you will never see in Boston. You must come to see us.

I love you and miss you,

Papa says that I can now take the letter to the general store.

Your grandson,
Steven Cocking, Jr

The heart of a 10 year old

Mr. Johnson had been transferred from St. Paul, Minnesota to a new post in Laos where they now have lived for a month. Mrs. Johnson was somewhat leery about the move and their son, Jimmy, age 10, was very unhappy having to leave his schoolmates and friends.

Jimmy came running home from school quite excited one day. "Mom, I just met our neighbor and he is an American just like us." This new tone of excitement surprised his mom. Jimmy had seemed so unhappy and withdrawn since starting school in this new environment.

"He's pretty old but he seems very nice," offered Jimmy.

"Yes, Jimmy, his name is Mr. Prince. He is with the US State Department just as your dad is," replied his mother. "He is a very nice man and I understand that he is about to retire. I'm sure you can learn a lot from him. He has been here in Laos for quite some time."

"Mom, I hate the school here. Dad made me go to the Hmong school. I hate it."

"Why don't you like it at school" his mother asked.

"I don't like the kids and I don't like the people here any better than I liked 'em at home," he replied.

"Why don't you call Mr. Prince and ask if you can come over to visit him this week end. He has been here for a long time and knows the Hmong people very well."

Jimmy came home smiling after his Sunday afternoon visit with Mr. Prince, with cookie crumbs still on his shirt. He sat down at the kitchen table as his mother prepared dinner.

"How was your visit," asked his mother.

"He asked where we came from and I told him St. Paul, Minnesota.

He said that I must have known Hmong kids. So many of the Hmong live in St. Paul," he said.

"He is so nice and kind and he knows a lot. It was kinda fun talking with him. I sure would like to visit him again," said Jimmy. A bond and trust developed between Jimmy and Mr. Prince after several more visits. Jimmy began to feel that Mr. Prince was more like a grandfather than just a neighbor.

"Why are you looking so glum?" asked his mother after Jimmy returned home from a visit with Mr. Prince. "You usually come home smiling and happy about your talks together."

"Well, he asked me why I didn't like the Hmong in St. Paul and why I don't like 'em here." A moment of silence.

"What did you tell him?" asked his Mom.

"I told him that the Hmong kids in St. Paul were stupid. They have funny names, they spoke funny English, they didn't understand what was going on, couldn't answer the simplest questions. They looked different, they kept to themselves, they never looked at you in the eye while speaking to you, and they are sissies. They don't stand up and fight. None of us liked them. I really gave them a hard time and told them to go back to wherever they came from."

"Wow," responded his mom. "I never knew that was going on."

"Not only that," continued Jimmy, "they don't like us here, so the few of us in the school from home keep to ourselves. They snicker when we speak, they laugh at how we dress. That is why I don't like it here."

"I can understand how you feel, son. But you usually come home so happy after your visits with Mr. Prince. Why so glum today?

"Mom, he told me about the Hmong. He said that a Mr. Vang Pao had traveled all over the villages in Laos a long time ago to ask men to fight with us against the Vietnamese. Mr. Vang Pao became their general. We promised to take care of them and give them rice and salt if they would help us throw the Vietnamese out. 30,000 volunteered and fought against the Vietnamese with our guys. Over 17,000 of them were killed in the fighting along with 5,000 Hmong civilians.

When our guys were pulled out of Vietnam, over 100,000 more Hmong were killed by what he called the communist Lao. Many fled to Thailand where they had to live in refugee camps for ten years. Many were moved to France and the US. Mr. Vang Pao led many to the US and he actually lived in St. Paul." Jimmy was almost breathless and as he repeated what Mr. Prince had told him.

"He told me about the customs of the Hmong, that looking away is a sign of respect, looking you in the eye is considered rude, that talking about yourself is often considered rude. They are apt to smile when told they goofed. In their culture it means that they are sad or embarrassed. The reason they often give for their action may not be the real reason. That is not lying to 'em, it's to avoid saying something disrespectful to avoid arguments."

Jimmy looked at the floor for a moment, then, eyes still downcast said, "Mom, that's why I feel kinda bad how I acted back in St. Paul."

His Mom put down the traditional Hmong white rice, meat and vegetable dish she was preparing for dinner, walked over to Jimmy and gave him a hug.

"Your father felt very bad about your having to leave your friends behind in St. Paul to come to Laos. He felt that it is important that you get to know that many people in this world are different than we are, that their customs and life styles seem as strange to us as ours look to them.

Few in our great country have yet to really experience and understand that. Tell your father about your conversation and how you feel when he returns from his trip to Thailand. I know how hard it is to tell someone you love that you were wrong. It is important that he hears directly from you how and why you feel as you do."

He looked at his mom soulfully.

She thought for a moment then said, "Now you know one must not be too quick to judge others. What can you do to feel better yourself, and to get along better at school?"

"I don't know." he responded with a dejected sigh.

"Well, think about it and when dad returns home maybe you, he, and Mr. Prince can visit to see what all three of you can come up with. We are proud of you, and we love you."

Jimmy snuggled close to his mother, quickly sat up and said, "Gee, dinner really smells good."

We are Moving Where?

"Guess to where we are moving." Kenny pompously announced to his fourth grade school mates. No one in his entire grade school had ever moved so far away. His proud bearing belied how sad he really was to leave his many friends. "Mom, this will be the blackest day of my life." he told her when she gave him the news a few days ago.

"Strange you should use those words, Kenny," she had answered. "It reminds me of what your great grandmother once said when she was in the fourth grade." She went to the book shelf and took out a book, her grandmother's memoirs. She gently blew the dust from its cover and showed it to Kenny. It was written by Kenny's great great grandmother in 1966 and its pages had begun to yellow with age. "Kenny read to me what she wrote."

He read; "My husband took a job on the West Coast which required our moving from our East Coast home. The day we moved, our daughter, who had many friends both at school and in the neighborhood, said to him, 'Dad, this is the blackest day in my life."

"Read on." his mother said. He continued: "A month after settling down in our new West Coast home our daughter had made so many friends and like it so much that she never wanted to leave our new home."

"I understand how hard it is to leave old friends, Kenny. But you see that new friends and adventures await you wherever you may go." his mother said. "Wait until your father comes home and he will tell you all about where we are going. We will be living in a biosphere on Mars."

"Wow. That's cool," exclaimed Kenny. He could hardly wait for his dad, a teacher at the local high school, to come home. Sitting around the kitchen table at dinner that evening Kenny bombarded his father with a million questions. Do any kids live there? How will we get there? Why do you have to go there? Can we still write to my friends here? Can we come back to visit?

"Kenny, many people live there and there are many kids of all ages." his father began. "That is why they asked me to move there. They need another teacher who can speak several languages and can teach both grade school and high school subjects. People from many countries have moved there and they all get along.

They want to learn to speak English. You will like it there. A space ship will fly us to our new home."

"But dad," Kenny interjected. "How can anyone survive there?"

"The biosphere on Mars is about as large as St. Paul, with parks, playgrounds, lakes and fun places to go. Scientists first started to learn what it takes to live in space about 150 years ago. A biosphere which covered over 7 acres was built near Tucson, Arizona, in which scientists lived. That proved that humans can live inside a biosphere which can produces all they need to live."

"But can I still use my I–Thought communicator to contact my friends here?" asked Kenny.

"Not only that," responded his dad. "Microsoft has developed a new I-Skype communicator and transmission antennas have been installed on Mars. You will be able to talk and see your friends here."

"Tell Kenny about what we decided to take with us on our move to Mars," interjected his mother.

"Yah, dad, can I take my though processor, automatic resource finder, and eye directed toys?"

"Yes, you can. However there is only enough room on the space ship for one piece of furniture. Your mom and I decided we would take this kitchen table. We always had mealtime at this table together with our parents which has meant so much to us when we were growing up. We always have these precious moments together at this table with you, to share the events of the day and to learn and discuss your cares and concerns. We want to continue this quality time and the tradition in Mars."

This knowledge of what is ahead had boosted Kenny's pride as he announced the upcoming move to his class mates. He even showed them a picture of where he will live.

"I'll send you my I-Skype password so we can still be close and I can show you something which is really fun and different," he said.

The Rusty Weather Vane

Tommy loved the outdoors. He looked forward to the weekends when he could ride his bike along the trails through the wooded areas and lakes around the city.

On a particularly beautiful weekend morning, he decided to vary his traditional route. Instead of riding along the city bicycle trails, he would ride down some of the now untraveled country roads seeking new discoveries.

As he started along the back roads, the flow of the fresh air galvanized his senses. He became acutely aware of the nature's beauty; the sun embraced stretches of wheat stirred by the morning's breeze; the fragrance of the countryside. He felt as though he was weightless moving through these beautiful scenes, a gentle breeze in his face.

He must have ridden along the rolling countryside for hours before spotting a tree on a knoll to which he slowly ascended. He sat comfortably against the tree to rest and eat the sandwich he had packed that morning. The warmth and serenity of the surroundings overcame him and he fell asleep.

Suddenly he heard what sounded like a rusty weather vane turning dolefully in the breeze. He followed the sound and discovered an old partially collapsed barn with its weathervane still attached to its tilted roof beam. An abandoned, deteriorating old house was located close to the barn. Tommy felt something eerily familiar about these structures. It was as though he had seen them before in much better and livable condition. How could that be?

He had lived in the city all of his life. Then he remembered he had been told that his grandparents owned a small farm before they sold out and moved to the city. Could it be that he had stumbled onto his grandparent's old farm?

He cautiously entered the front door which hung loosely on one hinge, the wooden floors creaking with each step. In what must have been a bedroom he found an old dresser. This damaged and dust covered old hickory dresser was leaning on only three legs and its mirror was broken. Tommy could not resist opening the two drawers each having only one remaining cast iron knob. The top drawer was empty except for a spider web. Then he spotted something stuck to the back of the bottom drawer. Carefully removing the item he was astounded by his find. It was a faded picture of his grandparents. Could his random bike ride and the sound of a rusty weather vane have guided him to his family's old homestead?

He continued to search through the dusty old house to see if he could find other relics of the past. A weird feeling continued to haunt him during his search when the sound of the weathervane grew louder and louder. Suddenly it stopped. A few seconds of silence then someone touched him.

He jumped with fright as the setting sunlight momentarily blinded his eyes. Standing in front of him at the base of the tree was a farmer. "Son, I saw you and your bike from below while I was harvesting my wheat and got concerned. You did not move for such a long time that I drove my tractor up here to see if you are alright." he said.

Tommy's head spun as awareness slowly returned to him. He wasn't sure how long he had slept under that tree but it must have been for some time. That was some dream, he thought.

"I'm fine," he answered, rubbing his eyes, "just thirsty."

"I'm through for the day," responded the farmer. "Come home with me and we'll have a cool drink and perhaps some of my wife's cookies."

"I hate to impose on you but I gladly accept your invitation. It's a long ride back to the city."

The first thing Tommy noticed as he entered the farmer's home was the old hickory dresser of his dream but in excellent condition. "May I ask from where you got this dresser?"

"Son, we purchased a small farm from a couple. This was in the house which stood on that property. The dresser was in bad condition but my wife liked it so we had it repaired. It was all that was left inside the house. We eventually razed the barn and house and converted the acreage to grow wheat." Tommy told him of his dream.

The farmer went over to the dresser, opened it and withdrew a faded picture. "We lost track of the couple in this picture from whom we bought the land, so could never return it. It was stuck in the corner of one drawer when we found it. Would you like to have it?"

The sound of a rusty weather vane had drawn him to the site of his ancestral home.

A Boring Vacation

The day was hot. The sky was grey.
We're bored to tears with nothing to say.
What a dreary way to spend the day
The whole vacation was one big ache.
Then suddenly….daddy fell into the lake!

Aroused from our stupor we began to laugh
As a duck bite daddy on the calf.
Go get the camera, hurry, quick
I snapped the scene, a clickedy, click.

The frolic from shore was fun to behold
As the tale in the lake began to unfold.
The ducks all quacked with sheer delight
And flapped their wings with all their might.

We all were laughing
And all came awake
The day that daddy fell into the lake.

The Explorer

John, 18 years old, loved to explore new vistas. His parents had encouraged his pursuit as he grew up and his self confidence had grown over the years. He had enjoyed taking unchartered day trips with no specific destination and took pleasure from the new discoveries along the way. He especially enjoyed the beauty of the flora and fauna and the quaintness of the small villages he encountered.

The anxiety at home mounted as the day approached when young son John would take the car for his first overnight vacation trip to visit his older brother Jim in a distant state. John was not familiar with the route but that did not bother him. He had a map and would stay wherever he could find accommodations along the way. That way he could meet new people. This had always added to the pleasure of his earlier one day excursions.

"John, it's not too late to make a hotel reservation for tonight," his father advised as John packed for the trip.

"Thanks dad. I don't want to be bound to a schedule. I like to explore the more scenic route and to stop wherever a vista or a quaint village attracts me along the way."

"Son, I packed some sandwiches, fruit, bottled water and cookies for you to take along the way" his mother said.

"Thank you, Mom. I'll take them but I like to get a meal along the way to taste the local cooking. I appreciate the food which may well come in handy. Otherwise I will take it to brother Jim's for us all to enjoy."

"Call us when you get there'" they called waving an apprehensive good bye.

The long ride though the countryside was indeed an exhilarating experience. The scenery was breathtaking and John spotted and recognized the wildlife along the way. As night time fell it began to rain and John could see lightning ahead. He began to search for a place to stay overnight.

The oncoming storm increased the urgency to find a hotel. He drove for miles through stormy weather and finally spotted a hotel in a small village. Suitcase in hand he ran inside through falling hail.

This hotel was the creepiest he had ever seen. The small dingy lobby, furnished with a few old well worn and frayed easy chairs, was not very inviting. He decided that the décor was 'Ancient Decrepit.' A small receptionist counter held a little bell with the sign, 'Ring for Help'. A peg board behind the counter held a few room keys. John tapped the bell and waited. Eventually a disgruntled, unshaven man in pajamas appeared, obviously annoyed by the interruption.

"Whatche want?" he asked. John, wet and tired, thought of an appropriate response but instead said, "I'd like a room for the night."

"Well, you'll havta pay ahead."

John paid and was given a key to a room on the second floor. The wooden stairs creaked as he carried his suitcase up the rickety steps. He entered the dimly lit room to find that its décor matched that of the lobby. An old bed with a sagging uninviting mattress occupied the major portion of the room. A single light bulb, suspended by a frayed electric cord, protruded from the ceiling. One old chair and a dresser, both well beyond their retirement age, restricted movement in the room. Next to a rusty sink was a ewer filled with cloudy water and a wash bowl.

It's a good thing that his mother had packed some food as there was no place to eat anywhere near and the storm was not weakening. He heard running in the hallway as he placed the food on the dresser. Soon the wind began to rattle a shutter on the window. Lightning provided an eerie light and the thunder was continuous. Then the power failed and the room fell into complete darkness.

The flashing lightning provided an eerie light. He heard a small child cry.

This was not going to be a very restful night. He shunned the sagging bed and decided to try to get what rest he could, still dressed, sitting in the chair.

The storm had passed as dawn brought its early light into the room. He quickly grabbed his suitcase and his mom's package and walked hastily down the creaky steps to his car. A man and wife with a small child also came out of the hotel to load their car which was parked next to his.

They engaged in conversation and soon discovered that they were headed in the same direction. The man suggested that they caravan to the nearest clean café for breakfast together. Their conversation at breakfast disclosed that the couple were not only friends of John's brother but also lived only a block from his home.

John followed the family using the quickest route to his brother's house.

His appetite for any further exploration had been dampened considerably by his experience…at least for that day. He had taken copious notes along the way. They would eventually add many pages to those already gathered for a future book.

THE MIDDLE YEARS

It All Started With a Kiss

That first kiss just blew me away. It was so fresh and delicious, so eye popping and smooth, that even the most dedicated aficionados must quiver in awe. I longed for more. What a way to celebrate the most joyous moments of one's life. Come to think of it, every day deserves a kiss. Surely one can never have too much. I heard that it has been enjoyed and shared generation after generation. It has been a favorite American treat since 1907.

Thank you Hershey's for your many flavored kisses.

Dancing

When I was in high school, I was on top of the world. I spoke English without an accent, thus was no longer 'different'. I played football and made the Kansas City all-star team; had an acting role in Charley's Aunt, the school play; was on the high school safety squad; and was elected to the national honor society. No longer an introvert, I had become a real 'big man on campus'... in my own mind.

At my mother's insistence I started to take a few dancing lessons. I loved the rhythm. This overcame my reluctance to attend the occasional school dances. I put on my sweater, adorned with a big football letter, and showed up to enjoy the next dancing event.

The music provided by the school band was great. Many of the popular girls also attended unescorted. They were soon engaged dancing with other 'big men on campus.'

When the next song started I asked one of the girls to dance with me but she excused herself explaining that she has a bad head-ache and was not feeling well. I returned to a seat to wait until the next song. I wasn't seated long when I saw her dancing with another fellow. That was a real putdown, a necessary wakeup call. So much for being a hero in my own mind.

My self confidence eventually rebounded sufficiently to strive to overcome this rejection. Continuing lessons significantly improved my dancing agility. I found a partner who enjoyed dancing who was so graceful that it was a real delight to dance with her. This was only one of her many charms which eventually led to our getting married.

During our honeymoon in Colorado we went to a restaurant which happened to have a small dance floor. We put a nickel in the nickelodeon and danced while waiting for our food. After dinner an elderly lady from another table came over and asked us to dance again. They enjoyed the grace of our dancing and had fed the nickelodeon for us.

We enjoyed dancing together for many years until the ravages of old age placed this pleasure into our treasure chest of wonderful memories to be opened at will.

She Opened the Door

In 1941 I began dating one girl more than others. My parents like her because she "could talk." She came from a very wealthy family although this was not a factor in our relationship. Her father had passed away years before and her mother worked as a chemical engineer.

World War II interrupted our relationship in 1943 although we continued to correspond. We continued seeing each other on my return from the service in 1946. I had an interest in chemistry which I intended to pursue at the University of Kansas. Her mother persuaded me to switch to chemical engineering instead. "Chemists are introverted people stuck away in a laboratory. You are too outgoing to be satisfied and to succeed as a chemist." she said. I was not persuaded by this reasoning but the more I looked onto chemical engineering the more I felt it suited my chemical, mechanical and space visualization aptitude much better. I switched.

When her mother sensed that my relationship with her daughter was becoming serious, she forbade her daughter to see me anymore. "He is an immigrant with no upward mobility. I want better for my daughter." (I had no car and streetcars provided our transportation.) That ended it. I was crushed. It took a while to get over it.

In the fall of 1947 a friend called. "Our group is having a picnic and one of the girls whom you may know does not have a date. Would you mind taking her?" Yes, I was aware of Barbara. We had attended the same High School. She was a freshman when I was a senior. Her cousins, who lived with their grandparents within a few houses where we lived, were among my best friends. I reluctantly agreed.

I had never experienced the pleasure and joy as I enjoyed with her at that picnic, how alive I felt. I had never met any who is so full of life that it could transport me out of the somberness and earnestness which my life's experiences seemed to have welded into my existence. She was fun to be with! I was never a good talker on the phone. Yet, I did not want our subsequent phone conversations to end. I began to see more and more of her and looked forward to the weekends when I could return from the University to see her.

I eventually asked for a date for New Years Eve 1947 but she had already accepted another date by that time. I immediately asked for a date the following New Years Eve and she accepted. We were married in August 1948.

Isn't it amazing that a woman who felt I was not good enough to marry her daughter opened the door not only to a satisfying career but also to the happiness I have known these last 66 years. She opened the door and there was Barbara!

The Good News

One often hears that troubles come in three's. Once a bad thing occurs it is almost sure that two others will soon follow. We now have evidence that wonderful things also come in three's.

Within 57 days three of our great grandchildren were born:

Theoren Leif on August 8,
Alivya Anna on August 27 and
Simon Guthrie on October 1.

That's good news. It reminded me of a young couple's experience. They lived in a lovely home nestled in the trees with a wonderful view of a small stream just down the road. An old wooden bridge across this stream provided the only access to their beautiful home. A real picturesque and serene setting.

They finally resorted to artificial insemination after all else failed to produce their desire to start a family. The eventual news that she was pregnant thrilled them both.

The wife's labor pain struck right on time on the expected delivery date. Unfortunately, a very heavy rainstorm also hit the area. It turned the stream into a raging torrent which damaged the bridge making it unsafe to cross.

At one o'clock at night, the terrified husband called the doctor. "Doc, what shall I do? The labor pains are one minute apart, the bridge is out, I cannot get her to the hospital, nor can you get here. Oh my god, she is screaming that the baby is about to arrive…Help!"

"Calm down," the doctor unruffled replied. "To start with, get a pan of warm water and a large warm towel. Help the baby come into this world, wash it, wrap it in the towel and place it near the fireplace where it will be nice and warm. That's all there is to it. Call me in the morning" The excited husband did as he was told.

As he laid the baby near the fireplace he heard his wife call, "Honey, hurry, there is another one coming." He rushed back, followed the procedure only to hear his wife call again, "There is another one on the way, hurry!"

Sure enough, she called again as he wrapped the second one in a towel.

"Oh my god," he heard her call. I feel another one coming." Breathless he rushed back to deliver number three.

When he heard her call again he shouted, "Hold it," and rushed to the phone to call the doctor. "Doc, you told me now to start it, now how do I stop it?"

The news of the frequent arrival of three new great grandchildren is so good, why stop it when they are on a roll?

Culture Shock

We live in a cocoon
Although we don't know it
Our habits, our gestures,
Our customs and language
Are a comfortable norm.
We live in a cocoon.

We visit abroad
Feel euphoria and excitement
Strange foods, architecture and customs
Are delightful discoveries
To later recall and relate.
We live in a cocoon.

But if we go there to live
We quickly are stressed
By an environment so strange
We become quickly annoyed
As the cultural shock takes its toll.
We live in a cocoon.

Is it appropriate to be pushed
By a woman in the subway?
Why can't we make friends?
Don't they like strangers here?
Why such unpredictable reactions?
We live in a cocoon.

We may become confused, disoriented
How should we communicate and act?

The obstacles of the culture around abound.
Uprooted from the comfort
We consider the norm.
We live in a cocoon.

Slowly however we adjust to the new
Our confidence builds as we adapt
To the differences and to view
Things more objectively and become
More flexible to a different norm.
We now live in another cocoon.

Our sense of humor returns
And we can laugh at ourselves,
We no longer say, "I'm stuffed" in Australia
For in that culture it means "pregnant."
No thumbs up in Chili where that gesture is vulgar.
What a different cocoon.

I do not send up a flare at a French restaurant
After waiting 45 minutes to receive a check.
Proper serving is their goal.
They did not resent my presence.
Table turnover is not a priority.
What a different cocoon.

Will cocoons around the world
Soon become a relic of the past?
As Facebook, Twitter, world travel and all,
Break the shells of cocoons around the globe?
Will all the cultures merge into one
And become one huge bland cocoon?

Changes and Shifts in a lifetime

Jim and Donna got together frequently with Bob and Mary. They had known each other since high school and long ago established a very comfortable and amicable relationship. They each had survived tragedies throughout their lives and in their middle age had become reflective about life. It was not unusual that they often shared their thoughts and viewpoints about life in general.

"Have you all wondered how life has changed you over the years?" asked Bob one evening.

"Strange you should ask that," replied Donna. "Jim and I look at ourselves and at our children and ponder how different we are today than they are. For example, we love our daughter-in-law for who she is, not for who she wants to appear to be. Where is the genuineness? Yet, when we think back to when we were at that stage of our lives, we remember that we sometimes donned a veneer."

"I've known you for a long time Bob. How life has changed you over the years. The perception we had at the time when you were the football star was that you were a self-absorbed, somewhat arrogant and assertive guy. These last twenty years I have come to know you as a selfless, sensitive and unassuming man," Jim offered.

Mary had been listening to this conversation very thoughtfully. It was evident that she had addressed the question of how and why life causes changes in our personalities and traits.

"Let me share my thoughts on how life seems to change us all," Mary interrupted. "I believe that within us all there is a balance being selfless and self-absorbed; being tolerant and intolerant; being genuine and superficial; being sensitive and insensitive; having integrity and at times 'bending the rules'; being humble and being haughty. Circumstances we encounter during our lifetimes merely change the balance between these opposites."

"You have obviously given changes we all encounter during our lifetimes some thought, Mary," Jim replied. "What do you feel are some of the causes for such a shift in the balance?"

"Perhaps I can answer that question and the one which Jim posed," Bob replied. "I can relate to Mary's theory. I believe that the environment at various stages of our lives tends to shift the balance between the opposites. When I played football, aggressiveness was valued. When I struggled to make a living for my family, I was more focused on my own needs rather than on the needs of others. I do not agree however that there is a balance between integrity and underhandedness. I can see no circumstance which can justify underhandedness. "

"Traumas we have all experienced in our lifetimes tend to make us more humble and change our lives," Donna contributed.

The discussion continued well into the night. All felt very comfortable of having reached a stage in their lives and in their relationships where they felt free to be true to themselves, to being understood and to be respected for their views.

The Voice Inside My Head

The voice inside my head is not my friend.

When I first wake up and want to go back to sleep, it says, **Get up! It is 10:00 in the morning already**. When a deadline looms for a major project and I handle trivial matters instead, the voice asks me **what in the world are you doing dummy? Don't you know that the report is due tomorrow?** What a pest that voice is!

Then when my mind seems to cloud over and I feel like a nap, there is that interfering voice again. **Get over it! Start to work and things will begin to clear up as you go along.**

When a friend brings over her favorite dish she concocted for us to taste and every bite seems like I'm being poisoned, the voice inside my head says, **Don't you dare tell her what you are thinking!**

When at midnight our visitors are still not finished telling us all of their illnesses and grievances and my eyes have glazed over to completely dim my hearing, again the voice in my head says, **Don't pass out, sit up straight, and nod in agreement. You're in no condition to be of help.**

I walk from the living room to the bedroom in a comatose state and instinctively stumble to bed at 1:30 AM.

Waking with a headache I turn to sleep some more when that intolerable voice again interferes and says, **Get up. It is 10:00 AM already.**

Down and Out?

He smelled of whiskey and despair
For months he had not cut his hair.
People around him would not strike a match
For fear this man on fire would catch.

People avoided him like the plague
For even his image was hard to take.
His scraggly beard, his messy clothes,
Added to the assault on their nose.

He was scrawny and he seemed quite tired.
The impression left nothing to be admired.
A troubled outcast from the human race
A dire future he seemed destined to face.

He had lost his job many months ago.
Then his wife left him which came as a blow.
His parents were killed in a car accident,
Losing his house, was a further entanglement.

He sat on a park bench lonely and shy
People walking by avoiding his eye.
When someone sat down right next to him,
Was this by chance or just on a whim?

"Pardon me," the lady said, "Is your name Kirk
Who worked at UPS as a shipping clerk?"
"Yes," he meekly replied quite surprised
While trying to keep his turmoil disguised.

"How do you know me and find me?" he asked.
She replied that it was really a major task.
"A friend of yours who knew your expertise
Helped my search and put my mind at ease."

"A job opening exists for a supervisor
To replace a retiring predecessor.
You are a top candidate for the position,
If indeed you meet the job's condition."

He cleaned up and gained rewarding employment
At a job which brought satisfaction and enjoyment.
And not only that, he married the woman
Who sat on the bench; they had much in common.

Fighting the Squirrels

Moving from our home at the edge of a wooded area to our condominium, I thought that my battles with the animals raiding our bird feeder would be over. The deer, squirrels, and raccoons could consume three pounds of birdseed overnight. Each animal presented its own challenge. This required replacements and adjustments to higher and higher technology birdfeeders, and frequent trips to the pet store to purchase more and different types of birdseed.

Bird feeders had been installed on a tree not too far from our large living room condo window. We enjoyed watching a great variety of beautiful birds, blue birds, finches, wrens, chickadees, grosbeaks and an occasional palliated woodpecker on the tree. Wild turkeys, also attracted by the bird seeds, added to the nature watching pleasure. The condominium caretaker fought the battles, we enjoyed the fauna. All of the fauna, except the ever present squirrels, disappeared when the bird feeders were removed.

My wife enjoyed gardening, a pursuit she undertook by planting various flowers and a beautiful decorative potted five foot tree on our patio. That started another battle with the squirrels. One day we found that something had dug out the dirt around the potted tree. A few days later we happened to see a squirrel digging up the dirt. A friend advised that mothballs at the edge of our patio would repel the squirrels. Unfortunately the squirrels could still penetrate this "mothball fence".

The counter tactic was to move the tree further away from an 8 foot high brick wall which provided some privacy for our patio, and to surround the tree with mothballs. A few days later we found that the entire tree was knocked over. Apparently, a squirrel had climbed the wall and jumped onto the top of the tree knocking it over.

Our battles continue. I will not be outsmarted by a squirrel. In the meanwhile however, we can't use the patio because of the strong mothball odor.

The Limits of Passion

Juan appeared to be a very intellectual, outgoing, good looking, and articulate fellow. Rhoda was a beautiful, gentle, romantic sort of a girl capable of strong emotions. They happened to be seated next to each other in a Western Civilization class at the University.

They began to date. Initially they double dated with another couple. Eventually Juan wanted to learn more about Rhoda so he asked her for a date to dinner at a very pleasant and quiet restaurant overlooking a beautiful lake. After a delicious dinner they sat on the deck overlooking the moonlit lake, soft background music floating over the tranquil scene.

"Wouldn't it be romantic if the song, '*A Sleepy Lagoon*' were to be played right now?" she asked.

"I would probably fall asleep right away." he answered

"Do you have a passion about anything?" asked Rhoda.

"Yes," he replied, "I have a passion about a number of things. I have a real passion for Western Civilization philosophers. For example, did you know that Malthus said that when the earth can no longer feed its growing population a catastrophe will strike? It will kill many in order to reduce the population to a number which the earth can support. For example, the black plagues in 1347 killed one third of the population of Europe."

He went on, "Malthus suggests that growing population rates would contribute to a rising supply of labor that would inevitably lower wages. He feared that continued population growth would lead to poverty."

That is not exactly what Rhoda wanted to hear. She had become quite infatuated with Juan and attracted to him.

"Any more personal passions?" she asked.

"Politics are my passion." he replied. He really became quite agitated and continued, "Politicians create problems and then campaign against them.

If both Democrats and Republicans are against deficits, why do we have deficits? If all the politicians are against inflation and high taxes, why do we have them?"

He became even more angry and louder as he continued, "The politicians in congress have the legal authority and power to enact laws, lobbyists don't. If legislators would spend as much energy doing what is best for the country as they do trying to convince us all what they did is not their fault, we would not have all these problems. "

He went on and on, finally concluding that, "We should vote them all out of office and clean up this mess."

The anger and his voice rose in response to her questioning his premises and pointing out the flaws in his conclusion. He accused her of being a part of the problem.

While Rhoda respected and admired a person for the passion they have for their belief or work, it quickly became obvious to her that even the physical attraction she felt for him initially crumbled. His unbridled passion had exceeded the limits of propriety.

My Magic Piano

Ella Fitzgerald singing, "I let a song go out of my heart. It was the sweetest melody I know. I've lost heaven' cause you were the song," kept ringing in Kevin's ears. Morning noon and night the melody haunted him.

He was surprised to see a piano sitting in his living room one evening after work. On its rack was the music sheet for "I let a song go out of my heart." He was so delighted that the question of how and why the piano appeared did not matter at the moment. He had always wished to play the piano.

Unfortunately, he could not read music or play the piano. No matter. He sat down and flawlessly played the entire score. It was pure magic. Wow, was he thrilled. Other songs popped into his head and he played these also. Kevin played any song which came to his mind. What a magic piano! He kept playing with great joy and sang along with the lyrics.

Suddenly he felt a touch on his shoulder. Everything was dark as he opened his eyes. He heard his wife's say, "Wake up. You were singing so loud in your sleep you woke me up."

However, he could not wait to retire that night to see what other magic awaited him. If several weeks in Hawaii, which keeps haunting him, can this also come true?

The doorbell awakened him the next morning. His wife rushed into the bedroom to announce that they had just won a two week vacation in Hawaii from Publishers Clearing House.

He could not wait to go to bed that night. He was on a roll.

Just for Today

Flying to New York on a sudden business emergency Jim, age 40, was desperately working on his laptop computer trying to prepare for the meeting ahead and to work on a report due the next day. Then his cell phone rang. It was from his secretary.

"You'll need to call the home office immediately. Your boss has been trying to reach you." No sooner had he hung up than it rang again. This time it was his wife. He could hear the kids screaming in the background. His wife sounded distraught. "The dishwasher is not working and I have the girls over for dinner and bridge tonight, what will I do?" Just then the captain came on the intercom,

"Ladies and Gentlemen this is the captain. Our flight has been diverted to Pittsburgh due to a mechanical problem. We will be landing there shortly. Further use of all electronic devices is now immediately prohibited until we land. Go to the check-in area near the gate to arrange for your next available flight to New York. Please fasten your seat belts."

Jim could feel his heart beat and the tension rising in the cabin as the stewardesses scurried around to assure compliance. "I'll call you back as soon as I can," he said before turning off his cell phone. As he turned off his computer, noticed a new message: 'Urgent, need immediate response.' In his hurry he did not think of saving the work he had done. A whole hour of work lost. Everyone was reaching him with issues which were not even on the horizon just 12 hours ago.

As the stress eventually ebbed during the four hour wait for another flight to New York, Jim began to ponder how much calmer and serene life was during his grandparent's days; no cell phones, no email, no airplanes which shorten travel time to relax disturbance free.

All of the time saving and communication devices have created a fast paced and stressful life. It would be nice, just for today, to live in yesterdays more serene environment. Yet, Jim reflected, all of these resources have enabled him to accomplish so much over such a short time all these years. They have made the quality of life he and his family have enjoyed possible. Couldn't we go back to yesterday just for today?

Mental Clutter

Chris had made a decision at work the previous day which could affect his future and had slept fitfully last night. Today had not gone very well either; his boss's anger at what may turn out to be a bad decision he had made, added to the stress. The drive home was a bummer. Traffic in San Diego was always congested but this was really bad. Stuck in traffic, his car was side swiped by a driver forcing his way into the merging traffic. He arrived home quite late and had a flat tire as he pulled into his driveway,

His wife met him at the door, angry that he was so late. "Don't you know that we have company coming tonight? The kids and I waited all this time to have dinner and our friends are due to arrive in half an hour to play bridge…" as a phone call for him interrupted the scolding. His mother-in-law was calling to ask why he did not send her a birthday card. Didn't he care?

As they sat down to dinner, the weather report interrupted the program to announce the threat of a late night tornado. That alarmed the kids. The door bell rang. It was a candidate running for office seeking their vote. By this time Chris was about to tell the candidate where to go, but he kept from unloading his accumulating angry stress on the candidate.

As they rushed through dinner which he could not finish, the sensory and emotional overload piled up. Bills waiting to be paid were accumulating on his desk, emails were waiting to be answered, birthday and anniversary cards for family and friends which should have been written and sent a few days ago were waiting for his attention. Will he still have a job in the morning, when will he have time to get the damage to the car and to his relationship with his mother-in-law repaired?

The bridge game turned out to be a disaster also. He held consistently poor hands and his distractions led to some poor playing on his part. This generated quite outspoken censures from his wife who was still angry about his late arrival home.

His life seemed to be like a continuous flow of unpunctuated sentences, unstructured and chaotic. He needed to bring some structure and order into his life. But how?

Then he remembered. A close friend who was experiencing similar stress told him of a Japanese garden near San Diego. He loved the Japanese friendship garden! He claimed that it brought peace into his life. Chris needed some peace, some way to handle the overwhelming stresses of his busy life. He decided to visit the garden the next morning after fixing the flat.

A sense of overwhelming peace and quiet overcame him as he stepped through the gate of the garden. It was almost a spiritual experience, as though he had stepped into something much bigger than himself. All the cacophony of the outside world was silenced. It was as though a peaceful and warm blanket of serenity enfolded him.

The bonsai trees, zen garden, the beautiful pagoda on the hillside approached by gently curving walks lined with colorful blooming flowers emitted a pleasant scent. The gentle waterfall caressed the rocks as it flowed into a calm pond filled brightly colored Koi seemingly floated like brightly colored flowers in the clear water. A wisteria covered wooden trellis adjacent to the pond emitted a pleasant and calming scent.

The serenity relaxed Chris. As he sat on a bench overlooking the sunlit pond he remembered that Thomas Edison once said, "The best thinking is done in solitude. The worst has been in turmoil."

He began to sort out his mental clutter, put each item into a separate box, close each box, and decide on the order in which he opens each one when he gets home.

He also decided to bring his wife, children and his mother-in-law to this beautiful serene garden next week end. Perhaps they too will put order to their mental clutter, and all will find harmony from the experience.

Perplexed and Regrets
A difficult Relationship

The family stood around his bed as Carl, age 97, peacefully drew his last breath in the nursing home in which he lived the last 11 years of his life. A stunned, respectful silence followed. Then his grandchildren began to softly cry.

Fritz, the only child of Carl and Rita, experienced a rush of emotions. His mother had passed away four years earlier at which time Fritz felt a terrible loss. Why could he not cry as his father passed away? It was as though he was looking at a complete stranger sleeping peacefully in the bed.

After a while he quietly asked his family to leave him alone with his father. He was struggling to sort out his emotions. Many memories of his father began to flood his consciousness as he sat in silence at the bedside of this complex man. Fritz's thoughts about his father drifted back over the years:

'You were strict, demanding and possessed a hair trigger temper. You demanded respect, immediate obedience, and tolerated no childish misbehavior. I began to fear the steely look in your eye which promised that severe punishment was about to follow.

Everything put on my plate had to be eaten before I was allowed to leave the table. Silent and sullen I once sat at the table refusing to finish the food which had been set before me. The punishment was a spanking and being locked in a dark closet.

You announced that you had entered me to run in a 1 kilometer race one morning. I had no idea what would be involved. Pain and breathlessness soon made me want to quit as others had done, but the consequences of quitting worried me more. I came in second, all others had dropped out. I was half a lap behind the winner. I fell to the ground weak and completely out of breath. "Get up! You are a disappointment." you said. You were never satisfied with anything I did to please you or what I was able to accomplish. Nothing was ever good enough.

My uncle took my cousin and me on a bicycle ride. We returned five minutes past the time I was instructed to be home. I was immediately spanked and locked in the dark closet despite my uncle's insistence that being late was his fault, not mine.

Two other events came to mind which affects my attitude. You insisted that I must earn a doctor degree before I can get married. It mattered not in what discipline. You had no idea of what I was studying and your eyes glazed over and you fell asleep if any discussion varied from the meat business. As I contemplated marriage you threatened that if I did not get a doctor degree first I would not get one penny from you. Thanks to part time jobs and the GI Bill, I had enough to fund my own education through graduate school and a Master's degree. By this time I had learned that my interests were so wide spread that being restricted to a very narrow specialty did not suit me at all. I also did not have the financial assets to continue for at least another two to three years. I silently vowed never to ask you for any financial help.

You continued to be demanding even after I rose to responsible positions in industry. You would call my office from the nursing home that you need help immediately, it was an emergency. If the line was busy, you would call the operator to report that this is an emergency and you need to be put through now. If my secretary told you I was in a meeting, you insisted that I be called out of the meeting. I have to come to the nursing home immediately. What were the emergencies? Time and time again it was that you had broken your electric razor and wanted it repaired immediately.

Various volunteer activities over the years had led to being elected chairman of the board of several nonprofit organizations. When you learned of this you advised me that it was the most stupid thing I ever did, that I am not capable of handling such important jobs

But, you had another side. Conditions beyond your control forced you into the business before you finished grade school. Yet, your mathematical skills were amazing. You could multiply, divide and add figures in your head faster than could later be done by slide rule and adding machine. You were a very skilled buyer of cattle. You could tell the weight, quality and quantity of meat a cow could produce within a few kilograms after a brief examination. You could process the meat into various cuts faster and with less waste than any other butcher.

A tornado had passed through the village destroying our home and the many meat related businesses which you owned. All of the facilities were reduced to rubble and left you without any insurance coverage. Fortunately we were not hurt as we had taken shelter in the wine cellar.

Most of the town laid in ruin. Essentially penniless and 40 years old, you got a job loading whiskey cases in the boxcars in another city where no one had heard of you. You earned enough to ensure that we had enough to eat and had a roof over our heads in a very small rented apartment. It was your courage, hard work, indomitable spirit and frugal lifestyle which over the ensuing years, allowed you to purchase a house and eventually a small grocery store which you and mother operated. You never borrowed one cent and would not purchase anything until you had the cash to pay for it.

There was one occasion, which permitted me to see that there was a heart and an emotional side to you. You had driven me to the bus terminal one cold and snowy night to board a bus taking me and others to the Army Induction Center at the beginning of World War II. Looking out the window as the bus departed, I spotted you running alongside the bus waving to me.

You were so different with your young grandchildren. You loved taking them out to dinner and when you saw that they liked their steak you ordered another one for them. Somehow not finishing what was set before them did not matter anymore. You laughed at their childish antics and enjoyed their energy and chaos. You admired their successes, the scratchy violin they tried to play, the piano tunes filled with "oops, I made a mistake."

Somewhere you did have a heart.'

Fritz was perplexed and was caught in waves of emotion. These last memories formed tears in Fritz's eyes and he softly said, "Dad, how much I wish I could have known you better, and that you could have known me better too. Rest in peace."

Forgiveness

Ann and Betty were close friends. They had known each other since grade school and went to High School and college together. This relationship had built trust which allowed both to share their most inner feelings. Each is good listeners, non- judgmental, intuitive, and compassionate. That relationship continued after they each were married.

Betty received a phone call from Ann one morning. Ann really sounded distressed. "Are you busy this afternoon?" she asked. "If not, I'd like to come over." A cup of coffee awaited Ann that afternoon.

"Ann, you sounded quite upset this morning."

"Yes, Betty, my husband said a hurtful thing this morning for which I will never be able to forgive him. Every time he does something which is hurtful, it opens up all the old wounds of prior hurts. I feel terrible."

Betty sat back as she tried to think about the response. Ann chose not to disclose what her husband said. She knew Ann loved her husband and that he loved her. She seemed to be searching for a way to keep these occasional distressing feelings from damaging her relationship with her husband.

"Ann, it is difficult if not impossible to forget the hurts we have experienced from someone we love. The answer I have found is forgiveness. Forgiveness does not change the past, but it does to enlarge the future."

"How can I do that when I feel so hurt?

"It isn't easy, Ann, I admit. I have found that if I begin to focus on the positive attributes of the one I love, rather than continue to focus on what has just happened, it helps begin the process of forgiveness. It helps if I take pencil and paper and write down all the joy and the wonderful things he has done for me over the years. The positives always outnumber the hurt of the moment. As I begin to simmer down, I also begin to wonder if it was something I might have said or done or neglected to do.

Did the stress of the moment cause my thoughtless act or comment? I look for the proverbial silver lining in the dark cloud. What I have learned from this has made me a better person and enriched my relationship with my husband."

Ann sat there for a moment trying to digest all that her friend had said. The self-discipline required to reach forgiveness at first appeared overwhelming. She took a sip of the coffee. She began to relax as the warmth of the coffee began to penetrate. Yes, she thought, I cannot let the event this morning destroy me or my relationship with my husband. It is certainly worth the effort to work towards forgiveness.

Betty noticed how Ann seemed to relax. Time to change the serious tone of this conversation.

"Ann, my husband once told me that when he was a kid he used to pray every night for a new bicycle. Then he realized that the Lord does not work that way. So he stole one and asked Him for forgiveness."

The Rose

Focused on my work, I did not notice that all had left the office for the night. I finished my deadline project, straightened out my desk and started for the door.

On the way out I noticed a beautiful red rose on the floor, still in full bloom. How did it get there? Did someone drop it accidentally? Did someone dispose of it to show their scorn? Is this a case of love lost? What do I do? Do I leave it there? Do I pick it up and take it home? I decided that it was so beautiful that it should be saved, at least until the next day.

I saw a glass on the desk of the only woman in our office, filled it with water, propped the rose into it and replaced it on her desk.

Returning to work the next morning I saw the woman fighting back her tears. The empty glass was on her desk, a drop of water clinging to its side as though even it had shed a tear. Her sorrow must be connected with the rose. Feeling compassion I told her how sorry I was and asked if she is alright.

"No," she sighed shaking her head sadly. "I lost my car keys and can't find them."

Yesterday, Today, Tomorrow

"Walter, you seem so calm and unperturbed by all of the turmoil in our country and the dangers with which we are faced in this world; how do you do it?" asked his old friend Ron.

"Why be concerned," answered Walter. "Think about it. In two days, tomorrow will be yesterday. You and I know that we can't do anything about yesterday. And today will already be two days old. Can we do anything about it? Of course not. So, why be so concerned?"

Ron just sat there stunned shaking his head not knowing what to say. Finally he asked, "Just what do you do each yesterday's today?"

"To start with Ron, I set the alarm clock the night before yesterday."

"Why in the world would you want to get up early yesterday?"

"I don't get up early. I just want the pleasure of turning it off and going back to sleep. You see, that is not something you can do were it not yesterday."

Ron began to have a feeling that he was sinking into a quagmire. 'Maybe I shouldn't ask Walter any more questions' he thought to himself. But Walter continued, "Then when I do wake up into two days ago I try to remember what I had for breakfast the day before. Trying to remember that at my age is quite a feat. However it is an exercise I go through to keep my mind active. You see, I don't want to have the same thing for breakfast every yesterday." This guy was quite coherent just a few days ago. Maybe I should try to change the subject.

"Walter, when are you going to see your grandchildren next?"

"In three days," he answered. "As you can see I have set the table to have lunch with them. You are welcome to stay as they will be here in just a few minutes."

On his way home Ron thought about how abstruse his fiend Walter can be. But Walter is a very bright guy. He finally concluded that Walter's message was, 'Don't waste your time worrying about things which you cannot control. Better to convert your energy to what is positive in the present.'

What was I Thinking?

"What, you did what?" Jan said dumb struck staring at her friend Jenny. Just then the sound of sirens and a knock on the door. Two armed policemen entered quickly scanning the surroundings.

The taller of the two said, "Would you both please sit down. Is there anyone else on the house?"

"It's all a big misunderstanding," Jenny blurted out nervously. "My husband and son live here but my husband left for work this morning and my son Jimmy left about 15 minutes ago. He is an actor and left for the theater."

Ignoring her the other policeman said, "Do you both live here?"

"No, I just came to visit a few minutes ago," said Jan still shaken by the sudden events.

"Where do you live lady and what is your name?"

Jan answered, "Jan Warren and I live near the grade school a mile from here."

The tall policeman turned to Jenny and asked if she owned a gun.

"Well, yes, but.." He quickly interrupted and asked her where the weapon is kept.

"It's in a drawer in the den cabinet."

Rising quickly he inserted his hands into latex gloves and assuring that his gun is handy ordered Jenny to walk to the den as he held her by the arm.

The other policeman stayed with Jan.

"What did you and your friend talk about?" he asked Jan.

Jan was afraid to answer. Jenny had told her that she shot Jimmy just before the police entered. Can she possibly tell the policeman that her friend had shot her son? Taking a deep breath and collecting herself she responded, "What in the world is this all about?"

"We had a report a few minutes ago that a shot was fired in this house."

Jan's mind worked feverishly. She cannot possibly tell the policeman that Jenny and she had a casual conversation when by this time all knew that a shot had been fired. That would make it look like she was trying to cover something up. Jan felt trapped. Reading Jan's body language the policeman sensed that Jan had been made aware something was wrong.

"Do you realize that the withholding of evidence could make you an accomplice to whatever may have occurred?"

Sensing that she had no choice Jan replied,

"Just before you came in Jenny told me she had shot Jimmy. But that could not have possibly occurred as I know that she loves Jimmy dearly and she would never do anything to hurt her son."

The policeman jotted her comments down in his notebook.

Entering the den, the tall policeman ordered Jenny to open the drawer of the cabinet and to step back. He carefully removed the revolver with his gloved hand and smelled the barrel. It had just recently been fired. He opened the cylinder and found only one spent shell in the chamber. Apparently there had only been one bullet in the gun when it was fired. He placed the gun into a plastic bag and then with Jenny in front of him they returned to the living room.

Something bothered the tall policeman. Something was not quite right. There was no sign of blood anywhere and it wouldn't have been enough time to clean up before the arrival of her friend Jan or their arrival at the door.

"What is the name, address and phone number of the theater where you claim your son Jimmy is in a play?" asked the tall policeman. Jenny produced the information which the policeman promptly texted to his headquarters asking that they immediately dispatch someone to the theater.

Within minutes the information came back to the tall policeman that Jimmy indeed is in the play at the theater and is not harmed.

"All right, Ms. Jenny, tell me what is going on here."

Jenny, shaking her head and almost on the verge of tears replied, "Just before leaving for the theater, Jimmy told me that in one scene of the play he was to be shot by one of the other actors. He had never been able to get his reaction time down to coincide with the sound of the shot. He had placed one blank into the gun and would I please shoot the gun that so that he could get one more practice before the opening of the play. Sounded silly to me, but playfully I went along."

The policemen, shaking their heads, left.

Jenny, shaken by the events she had set into motion, sank deep into the sofa and said to Jan, "What was I thinking?"

THE (G)OLDEN YEARS

Rejuvenation

Two old friends, each in their 80's, were reminiscing about how long they could each live. They both were in pretty good shape, one still playing tennis, the other still enjoining rounds of golf.

"You know, Tom, Methuselah lived to be 969 years old. There ought to be away for both of us to live that long also."

"Jerry, you must be dreaming. No one has lived that long. Not since that appeared in the Bible for Methuselah."

"I sure can't argue that fact, Tom. However I have recently learned that one of the leading non-profit organizations supporting scientific research which aims at life extension is the Methuselah Foundation. They have achieved several breakthroughs. They have extended the life of mice two and a half times and have rejuvenated mice. These developments give hope that scientific means are available to delay aging and extend human life in the foreseeable future."

"Yes, Jerry, I also happened to see a report on BBC and later read in Fortune magazine that the Foundation has awarded prizes to those whose research has effectively extended the life span of mice to unprecedented lengths.

However, I would not like to be turned into a mouse in order to live longer."

At This Stage of the Journey

Jim, age 86, was a little nervous. Sitting across the coffee table from him in the studio was a reporter from the local TV station about to interview him. This was first of the TV station's new 'Golden Age' program series. The interviewer opened the program.

"This is Drew Cramer. The number of Americans over age 65 is soaring. In 1950 8.3% of the population was over 65. This rose to 12.3% by 2000 and is projected to rise to 21.1% by 2050. By 2030 they'll number 71.5 million, one in every five Americans, twice the number in 2000.

The number of Americans age 85 and older will rise to 9.6 million, about double the number in 1990. This population is healthier, more active and vital today than ever. Many work well beyond the age of 65 and many over the age of 75 are actively pursuing various hobby, education and social activities. During this series of programs we will cover a variety of subjects relating to this aging population. Today we would like to focus on how one octogenarian views the current stage of his life's journey. We are happy to welcome Jim Deriter."

"Jim, I'm intrigued by your last name. Spelled backwards it reads *retired*," said Cramer trying to put Jim at ease. "Did this forecast that you would back into retirement reluctantly?" This brought a smile to Jim's face.

"Never thought about it in this way, but I did retire with some trepidation'" Jim answered.

"When you were born?"

"In 1924," came the answer.

"Before we get to your view of the current stage of your life Jim, tell me about some of the stages you remember and what were your hopes along the way."

"The earliest I remember was at age 5 or 6. I wanted to be a truck driver and a football player."

"And did you realize these dreams?"

"These were a child's vision of exciting and fun things to do. I did play football in High School and college. Soon however reality set in. I met the dream of my life and got married. At that stage of my life I needed to concentrate on a career to support a family."

"I see from your memoirs that you did have a very successful career. During that stage in your journey through life, what was your focus?"

"Establishing a home for my growing family and learning how to become a parent to our four daughters. Both were a challenge." answered Jim. "Another focus crept in during the more financially comfortable later twenty years of my career. My job required extensive travel around the world including living abroad for 3 years. While I was always grateful to our country, this made me acutely aware just how exceptional it is. As a result I became increasingly involved serving on various volunteer organizations in my spare time."

"Considering the exhilaration provided by the responsible positions you held both professionally and with volunteer organizations, I can see that retirement could cause some anxieties," said Cramer.

"During my 44 years employment I had accumulated a wealth of experience. I really wasn't ready to retire at age 65. I searched for a way to apply the experiences I had acquires in some productive manner. It did require some time to adjust to the change and to reset my sails."

"Did you find other employment at age 65?"

"No. No one would hire a 65 year old retiree. I continued my volunteer work at a level which provided some challenge and which utilized my experiences to a degree, but I needed more. After a while I decided to start my own consulting company. I managed this operation for another nine years after which I did retire.

"What is your point of view now?" asked Drew Cramer.

"My problem with retirement is that there are no weekends off. I am busy seven days a week. This is quite the opposite of what caused my trepidation about retirement. I need not have been concerned."

"What keeps you busy?"

"I've always had an interest in our family genealogy, photography, and writing my memoirs. Genealogy research, selecting, upgrading and digitizing thousands of slides taken over the years, taking pictures during the many family celebrations, and enrollment in a creative writing class has been most edifying and challenging.

In addition, I have always wanted to do more reading. I have started a bridge group with other retirees which we enjoy. The computer opens up a whole new world to explore. TV allows you to watch historic events all around the world unfold as they occur. There is so much more to learn and the tools to do so have become so much more accessible. It is quite exciting. It's like being a kid suddenly finding himself in a candy store with an overwhelming assortment of free candy. There isn't enough time to enjoy it all."

"Any advice to the upcoming 'deriters?'"

"I am a little reluctant to give advice since every situation is different. An old friend of mine answers this question with "Don't get old." I realize that advanced age can be accompanied by limiting health and mobility problems. Multitasking may no longer be a strength. One's numerous experiences may not find a direct and rewarding application. There is concern that the rest of your life will be filed with trivialities. This can cause initial anxiety along with the trepidation of boredom. This concerned me also.

I suggest to that you relax and enjoy the boredom for a while. You will need some time for yourself. Soon however realize that you have not lost anything at all. The world is filled with an exciting and overwhelming variety of candy for you to sample and to enjoy. You'll soon find that you have no weekends left at all."

It's Never too Late

Harry and Bob are good friends. They shared their private thoughts without fear that these would threaten the depth of their friendship. This seemed unlikely as Bob was the eternal pessimist and Harry was such an optimist. Both are very capable men and had retired from successful careers. Harry was busier than ever pursuing many projects for which time was not available while gainfully employed.

"I am truly bored. The transition from a hectic and challenging job to suddenly sitting at home, with make do trivial activities just to pass the time, is really getting to me," Bob said to Harry one day. "I have a hard time fighting off depression. I am always 'on stage' pretending all is wonderful when deep inside it really isn't. Your job was equally challenging and retirement also occurred suddenly. How do you stay so upbeat?"

Harry pondered the question for a minute.

"Bob, you used to take such great pictures many years ago. I remember your taking a great picture of our grandson when he was born. It is still hanging on our refrigerator and we are proud to show it to our friends. Can you imagine that he is now an attorney and is about to present us with a great grandchild? Have you thought about taking up this hobby again? You enjoyed it and it brought such joy to others?"

"It's too late, Harry. My camera is old, 35 mm film is almost impossible to obtain and to have developed."

"The new digital cameras are just great," said Harry. "They are small and have become quite inexpensive. You can stick them into your shirt pocket and they take absolutely wonderful pictures which you can print out on your computer within minutes. We won't have to wait a month to get a copy of our expected new great grandchild!"

"Yes, I know," answered Bob. "But there is so much to learn. All of this new technology is a hassle to learn."

"Try it, Bob. You used to be invigorated by new challenges during your most successful career."

They met again several weeks later.

"Harry, you'll never know what happened. I thought about what you said and went out and bought a digital camera. There was a brief testing and learning time. After that a whole new world opened up for me. Taking pictures outdoors began to make me so aware of the beauty all around us. I never saw the fall colors in such magnificent display or the sky so blue. Some friends saw some of my pictures and asked if they could have a copy to frame."

He continued. "My wife and I now plan to travel around Lake Superior during the fall on a photo expedition. Our son tells us that the scenery along the way is absolutely breathtaking and the views so varied. Your great grandchild will have to wait for his picture until we get back."

It's never too late to learn, mused Harry with delight.

A Hole in One

"It seems like it was only yesterday that I was young, just married and embarking on a new voyage with my mate," said Dennis to his old friend and golf partner Charley. "Yet it seems eons ago."

"I know what you mean." replied Charley. "I too wonder where the years went. There are the glimpses of how it was back then with all of my hopes and dreams."

Dennis nodded in agreement.

"Life has caught us by surprise, Charley. Here we are on the 'back nine'. How did we get here so fast?"

"I remember seeing older people thinking they are awfully slow and withdrawn." Charley replied. "I am only on my 'first hole' and the 'back nine' are so far away that I could not possibly imagine what it would be like. They are the folks we used to see and never thought we'd become."

After a moment of reflection Dennis replied, "Just getting a shower is such an ordeal and taking a nap is not voluntary, it's mandatory. If I don't take it, I fall asleep where I sit. I sure was unprepared for all of the aches and pains, and the loss of strength to do things I need to do. I know I'm on the 'back nine' but don't know how far along. Have you ever thought about this, Charley?"

"Yep, sure have, but I have no regrets. I've not achieved all the goals I set while on the 'front nine', but I know I did the best I could. That is what I want my loved ones to remember. I hope they appreciate the love I have for them and recognize all I have done for them in years past. Meanwhile, Dennis, let's us live and enjoy each day well. Who knows when the 18th hole has been played? There is still so much more to accomplish toward the goals we have set. Remember the hole in one you shot ten years ago? Perhaps another one still in sight,… off the golf course."

Ode to Susan on her 60th Birthday

September 24 is a special day on which
We travel down memory lane.
An event occurred which did vastly enrich
And bring joy thought impossible to attain.

Your quick arrival surprised us all
Including the Coffield physician,
And I quickly made a long distant call
To advise family of this miracle addition.

From early on with energy abounding
Running, not walking wherever you went
Your broad interests were really astounding
An omen of things to come we were sent.

The move to Wichita you took easily in stride
Making new friends along the way
Always seeing the positive side
Bringing sunshine into every day.

Your leadership skills became apparent soon
As you led your sisters in play
And continued throughout your high school commune,
You were certainly well on your way.

Homecoming queen elected by your peers
And a developing friendship with Dave
Promised much more in the coming years
For the record which you would engrave.

Speeding down the road through the ensuing years
You have touched and improved many lives.
You have helped many friends, family and peers
The quality of living you've enriched and revived.

Beloved daughter with whom we are blessed,
May your road ahead be smooth and straight
And may your wisdom in your descendents nest
And may your joys never ever abate.

Happy 60th Birthday

Feeling Old

I've reached the winter of my life and it caught me by complete surprise. I still have a full deck, I just move around slower now. I have come to realize that a person's age is something impressive, it sums up one's life: maturity reached slowly and with the help of many obstacles; illnesses cured or controlled; grief and despair overcome; risks unconsciously taken. Maturity is formed through so many desires, hopes, regrets, forgotten things, and loves. It has accumulated a fine cargo of valuable experiences and memories. It seems just yesterday that I was young, just married and embarking on my new life with my mate. Yet in a way, it seems like eons ago, and I wonder where all the years went.

A lot of assumptions are made about aging. Most of these assumptions prevent connection and knowledge sharing. Assuming that all old people are technically incompetent, that they are deaf or stupid, that they are old grouches, all are unhelpful generalizations.

We are still unique individuals, with the same range of values, gifts, and flaws as any other person. Many of us are rediscovering lost hobbies, roaming the world, grappling with life's great mysteries and spending time learning new things which astound us.

Just the other day a young person asked me how I felt about being old. It took me by surprise for a minute as I did not consider myself as being old. Yes, I sometimes despair over my body and am taken aback by that old person that lives in my mirror, but I don't agonize over those things for long.

Then I remembered Bob Hope's answer, on his 100th birthday, to how it feels to be old.

"At age 70 I still chased women, but only downhill.
When I turned 80 even my birthday suit needed pressing.
At 90 I knew I felt old. The candles cost more than the cake.
At 100 I don't feel old. In fact, I don't feel anything until noon.
Then it's time for a nap."

Apparently age is only a number if you retain your sense of humor.

Getting Old

Sometimes I now begin to feel
That I'm really getting old.
How quickly the time has gone.
How did this feeling unfold?

There is still so much to do;
New demands seem never to slow
Am I now too old to follow through?
My mind says no but my body says whoa.

When 20 I served in World War II
I took risks which now make me cringe.
But at that young age I had no clue,
I fought for my country, I was on a binge.

By age 30 I had a family to support,
A future to build for our growing brood.
Hard work, but there was still time to cavort,
With boundless energy I was imbued.

At 40 with drive and energy in full bloom
I searched for more chances to contribute.
There's still more vigor available to consume
With help for many others to distribute.

Blessed during my 50's with some success
And still seeking to undertake more,
I accepted challenges drenched with stress,
I strode into ventures with problems galore.

Armed with experience gained over previous years
In my 60's I took yet another large risk.
And with the help of some valued peers
I ran my own company for another 8 years.

Along with this effort I held volunteer positions
With organizations which were in a state of transition.
Now in my nineties I do still yearn
To handle challenges of major concern.

But reality stares me in the face.
I'm really no longer in the race.
The candle of energy has burned near its end
With what I can still do and have done I'm content.

It Takes a Little Oil

Getting up in the morning and facing a pile of accumulating paper work is like trying to start a lawn mower which has grown rusty due to long disuse. I grunt and groan, then see a grumpy old man in the mirror who would stall any engine.

I head to my desk and pull the rope to encourage my mind to start. I push and pull and finally get the beast to nudge forward.

It takes until mid morning to get the old motor running enough to begin mowing down some of the paper work and the projects awaiting my attention.

When interruptions divert my path, the mowing becomes spotty. This creates another pile of paper. By evening papers, old and new, lay strewn across my desk in disorder creating yet another pile I need to mow down, well, perhaps tomorrow.

What really oils the motor and makes it hum is completing a whole row to mow, that is, finishing an entire project. Wow, does that feel good!

A drape over the mirror also helps.

A Curve in the Road

Two old business friends, Sam and Harry, sat in the sun room of a nursing home one afternoon watching the traffic on the street below. They often sat there sharing memories, discussing business strategies, various philosophies, and commenting on the daily news.

"Harry," said Sam, "did you notice that new cars way outnumbered the old ones? I hate to think how many old car part suppliers have gone out of business. I wonder if any of the old car market manufacturers had the flexibility and the persistence to survive."

"Sam, there is a thin line between persistence and stupidity. An old friend of mine who owned several large typewriter stores was determined to have his business survive as technological changes occurred. He was persistent and learned how the computer can increase his customer's profitability. He started selling computers as his typewriter business began to decline." Harry commented.

"One of my friends in the typewriter business was equally persistent, Harry. As sales began to decline he increased his advertising spending, reduces staff, work longer hours himself, and tried to negotiate lower prices for the typewriters bought from the manufactures." Sam responded. "He was persistent and worked hard. He defended his sticking to his old typewriter business by pointing out that his business had grown very well over many years. I tried to tell him that you cannot drive down the road looking only into the rear mirror. That is great as long as the road remains straight. When you encounter a turn, and no road in life or in business is ever straight, you will surely wreck the car."

Harry agreed. "His business failed because it was not prudent to maintain a business that clearly had no future. Look what happened to the buggy whip business. No matter how persistent those business owners were, buggy whips have disappeared from the scene. You know, that may be a good subject to raise with our own grown children. They are doing very well in a fairly stable economy. Are they prepared for a curve in the road?"

Motivation

"Bernie, we've both enjoyed a long life which had many aspects for which we are thankful," commented Jim. "We have had such a great quality of life. I am most thankful. However the world news and the national news are so depressing today, I begin to believe our grandchildren may experience a much lower quality of life and may live in a tinderbox world. I am concerned that they will not be able to enjoy many of the things for which I am most thankful."

"I too am grateful for so many things, Jim; having escaped the worst of the Holocaust, survived the dangers during combat in WWII, having been given the opportunity for an education and for upward mobility, for the opportunity to return, in a meaningful way, the benefits I have received from my community and my new country," replied Bernie.

"That is a sizable list, Bernie." Jim nodded. "Is there one thing, which you can control, for which you are most thankful?"

"I'll have to think about that for a minute."

Bernie sat silent for a minute and then replied: "Perhaps having strong motivation to overcome obstacles which block the way to a successful outcome is an aspect for which I am most thankful."

"I don't understand, Bernie. What do you mean?" Jim asked.

"Many years ago I saw the poor conditions under which the intellectually disabled individuals, then called 'mentally retarded', were warehoused," Bernie replied wistfully. "I returned to my home and saw my four healthy children. I vowed to someday thank the power which granted me this blessing. I was motivated to do something.

Over the years of my industrial life and my volunteer experiences I learned much more about the abilities of the millions of tax funded, warehoused intellectually disabled in our country. I also became aware that various industrial segments, like the hospitality industry, need the abilities of these individuals to solve major turnover problems.

Strong objections were raised to a program I proposed to train and place them in hospitality industry jobs. Unions, the industry, to a degree by parents of the handicapped, and by a significant portion of my employer's top management who had become aware of my outside activity, all opposed it. Special training would be required to enable the intellectually disabled individuals to fill the various positions. Housing near the industries facilities was not available and transportation, from the distant facilities warehousing these individuals to the urban jobs, did not exist. These were significant obstacle to overcome.

Four years of my spare time were spent working to overcome these obstacles. The Minnesota Department of Vocational Rehabilitation became a key partner.

The breakthrough finally came when 10 such individuals placed at a well know hotel exceeded all expectations, performance, and savings projections. By 1970, 2000 individuals were employed by the hospitality industry in Minnesota. The program was expanded nationally. Requests to install it abroad were being received. Tax recipients were made tax payers and most of all, the self image of intellectually disabled grew as did public recognition of their capabilities. The doors of the warehouses began to open! The program received the Presidents Distinguished Service Award.

I am thankful to this day for the opportunity to make good the vow I had made many years ago to express my gratitude for four healthy children in such a significant way. I was motivated to overcome significant obstacles. Motivation is at the top of my list."

"You know, Jim," Bernie added, "There are millions of individuals in this great country of ours who also devote their time and effort to address difficult local, national and international challenges. They are motivated! That makes me optimistic that our grandchildren will not have to suffer a hard and fearful life."

What is Most Important?

"Jerry, what is most important in your life?" Greg asked his close friend.

Jerry had sensed that something was bothering Greg but this question caught him by surprise. He sat back in deep thought for a minute, his mind racing for a thoughtful answer.

"Greg, that is such a profound and meaningful question. It is not a question which I ever thought about during my life time, yet I must have subconsciously chosen my priorities and made decisions which conformed to what was and is most important. Is something troubling you, Greg?"

"You put your hands on it, Jerry. Personal problems, family problems, financial problems, local, State, Federal and international problems, environmental problems, security issues, crime, terrorism, and many other conditions overwhelm me. I'm overwhelmed and perplexed! You seem to be so laid back, Jerry. How do you sort all this out?"

"I'm no wizard, for sure, and the many problems can indeed become overwhelming. In addition, our priorities change as we travel down life's highway," responded Jerry.

He added: "For example, being an only child with very busy parents, the most important thing at that early age was to have play-mates. I was bored. Later, the most important thing was to get an education. Marriage and children made my family and earning a living the most important.

Now at an advanced age, the many situations which you have identified have started to compete and befuddle me; problems with grandchildren, financial management to keep our head above water, environmental, crime, security versus privacy issues, international issues, etc.

What I try to do first is to determine which of the many issues I cannot control.

I try to keep abreast of these issues, such as the international problems, the seemingly irresolvable stalemate problems within our various governmental authorities, gun control, abortion rights, crime, global warming, etc. These I put in boxes, and lock them tightly and set them aside.

Are there issues which hopefully I can influence? Yes. For example, resolution of family problems. If not leading to immediate success, these can be but into box to be opened when opportunity arises.

What can I control? Handling my health issues, managing our finances, optimizing the quality of our lives, selecting my social contacts, pursuing further education, helping others who cannot help themselves, all are activities which I can and should control. These rise in importance. Greg, it sounds like a simplistic answer for such a meaningful question. It isn't easy to implement but in retrospect, it helped me prioritize and to stay remain calm in what has always been a chaotic world."

Ode To my Beloved wife on
Our 63rd Anniversary

Each year on this date I strive to tell you
The love and appreciation I so deeply sense
For all that you are and for all that you do
Makes my striving even more intense.

Although old age has taken its toll
And I wish I were whole again,
My love and passion remains totally whole
When I hold you I feel no pain.

The touch of your hand calms my turbulent seas
And your smile brings sunshine galore,
The storms are reduced to a gentle breeze
And into the sunshine my heart starts to soar.

My love is unfaltering through the occasional storm
Which no marriage can ever transcend
For intelligent people it is quite the norm
But know I will love you to the very end.

An Old Spouse's Love

I just want to know if you're proud of me
I want you to see what's inside of me,
What quietly all the pain I go through
Of which you do not seem to have a clue.

My smile hides that I am calling for help
I'm a ghost without casting a reflection.
It's as though I don't exist in your life
My need for you is beyond your detection.

I want you to support me when I'm not my best,
I know that sometimes I am the problem too.
You need your outside friendships for fun and the rest,
But I too need quality time to spend with you.

As days go by nothing seems to change.
Your demeanor is cold and combative
Which prevents a rational interchange
And makes my life so unattractive.

I dream of what our life could be like
If the support and love of our early years
Could cause my spirit again to rise and spike
And add years as it stills my silent tears.

I am deeply in love with you, my memories are still fresh
Of all you have done to create such happiness.
I am so proud of you and shout to the world
Of your talents and all you do lest it is unheard.

I pray to the lord that you are alright and I suffer your every pain
But the time is growing short again make something of this,
For our old love, compassion and closeness to regain
To spend the rest of our lives together, living in tender bliss.

Old but the Flame Still Glows

He looks out of the window and see the trees waving sadly back to him. Their leaves are falling, blown by the winds which bring on the winter. Soon they will be bare.

Some trees will survive the winter and regain the grandeur of their past. Others will struggle through the coming spring and summer, never to regain their splendor. Some will not survive the frigid winter's snow and ice with which they will soon be coated, their roots not refreshed by sustaining water before the frost to grant them another year.

The scene generates some strong and sad feelings within him. His life is like the cycle of the trees. No longer does he look to regain the splendor of the past. Each new season has become a struggle, laden with a heavy blanket of loneliness and isolation, without the refreshment of compassion and understanding.

The phone rings and it is a long distance call one of his grandsons. He is awakened from his stupor by the joy from this call. He realizes the richness with which the years have rewarded him, the many tasks still awaiting his attention, the freshness of the great experiences he has been granted. It may be winter outside, but inside the flame still glows.

Real Love

A very wealthy old couple had three grandsons. The old grandfather wanted to find out just how much his three grandsons really love him.

So he took a walk with the oldest and faked that he tripped and fell into the river. The grandson immediately jumps after him and pulls him out of the river. The very next day he sees a brand-new Ford in front of his house with a note attached to the windshield. The note said, "Thank you for saving my life! Your grandfather."

The next day he repeated the same act with his second grandson. He fell into the river and this grandson saved him as well. The next day he sees a brand-new Chevrolet on his driveway with a note which said, "Thank you for saving my life! Your grandfather."

The grandfather was obviously very excited to see how much is two grandsons loved him. He still had one more to test. So he went for a walk with his youngest grandson and again fell into the river. The young kid didn't even vary his stride. He continued his walk and went back home. The very next day he saw a brand-new Mercedes in front of his house with a note which read, "Thank you for saving my life! .... Your grandmother."

Now that is real love.

What is Passion?

Passion is a feeling warm
which in my youth was quite the norm.
But as I aged, much to my bane,
it seems to be quite on the wane.

That's not to say it's gone away.
Occasionally it still has its ubiquitous way.
It's been replaced by enthusiasm nifty,
which of course, is much less risky.

Projects long in memories storage,
upon these I have now begun to forage.
Composing my memoir, and creative writing
I now find to be fun and quite exciting.

These keep the spirit gently soaring,
providing challenges far from boring.
Much to my surprise I've just discovered
that passion and enthusiasm are closely mirrored.

The only thing which has now changed
is the object on which my passion is rained.

What is Love?

Nobody really knows what love truly is. Most side step the question. Answering the question, "What is love?" seems to be something with which we have difficulty. So, of course, this writer in true Don Quixote fashion (quoting Cervantes, "Finally, from so little sleeping and so much creative writing, his brain dried up and he went completely out of his mind") rushes in to answer it.

There is love for a child, puppy love, sexual love, spiritual love, love which elderly couples feel for each other, love of sports, movies, love for ice-cream, cake, pizza, etc. They are all different yet they are all called love. A five year old once asked her older brother, "What is love?" one day. He answered, "Love is when you steal the candy from my school pack every day….and I still keep it in the same place."

Many believe that love is a sensation which is magically and spontaneously generated, based on physical and emotional attraction, when Mr. or Ms. Right appears. Just as easily however it can also degenerate when the "magic just isn't" there anymore. Sages over the centuries have indicated that true love has five components, care, responsibility, respect, and knowledge, and commitment. Sounds pretty clinical for such an emotional experience so some elucidation is in order.

> **Care** is demonstrating active concern for his or her life and growth.

Responsibility is responding to his or her expressed and unexpressed emotional needs, (particularly in an adult relationship.)

Respect is the ability to see the person as he or she is, to be aware of the other's unique individuality and wanting that person to "grow and unfold as he or she is".

Knowledge allows one to care for, respond to, and respect the other only as deeply as one knows the other.

Commitment to one another will see only the positive when faced with seemingly negative information about the partner. For example, if a friend comments that your partner doesn't say a lot you reply, "Ah, yes, he is the strong silent type."

Don't say, "Yeah, I can never have a conversation with him. It's annoying."

Now how do sports, movies, ice cream, cake, pizza, fit in? Well, just as with a person we love, when they are not available, we miss them.

Quiet Chaos

"We'll have 31 over for our great granddaughter's birthday party," my wife informed me. My first thought was about the chaos our 5 great grandchildren ages one to six have caused in the past, crying, running around wildly, spilling food and scattering toys like booby traps waiting to explode as adults try to circulate in the fairly close space. Their parents fully engaged in conversation with their peers blissfully ignoring the conduct of their children. Joining this cacophony were the many voices, all speaking at once above the din raising the decibel level above the limit permitted by OSHA.

"Aren't they a beaut?" I thought I heard an older friend say about the little ones above the noise level piercing my hearing aids as I stepped on a piece of birthday cake on the floor. I wasn't sure, could she have said "Aren't they cute." How I answered depended on just what she said. I decided to just nod in reply.

I felt isolated, unable to circulate, unable to hear above the noise and to participate in the conversations. The building crescendo eventually made my head spin, forcing me to seek refuge in the quiet of my room.

Slowly, as I gathered myself, another thought crept into my consciousness. How blessed I am to have such a great family, children, grandchildren, great grand-children and friends. How wonderful that they stay together, get along so well, and enjoy each other's company. Was I any different at their age? But how could I, at their ages, have understood, or how can I now expect them to understand the conditions which old age imposes.

After a while I returned to the turmoil in time to see the birth-day child open her presents. The joy in this child's eyes and the smiles on the faces of my children and grandchildren also helped to quickly quiet the chaos in my mind. I settled back to enjoy the moment with serenity.

I was ready for another round.

Who am I?

It's very quiet here,
Though the birds sing their song
Not one sound do I hear,
I am lonely, I don't belong.

That mantle of loneliness is heavy
And I've worn it for so long
It's imposing a burdensome levy
What has gone so wrong?

It's hard to keep on smiling
And to think of life as a song
When my loneliness keeps on pining
For a kindred spirit I very much long.

No friend is near or within sight
With whom to share my dreams,
There's no relief, come day or night,
My destiny is doom it seems.

The stem which held my head so high
Is rapidly losing strength.
It searches for nutrients from roots all dry,
I am much shorter by several lengths.

"The air is so strong it takes my breath away,
So all I do is cry all day.

Who am I?
I'm a lonely little petunia in an onion patch
My eyes really burn with every breath I catch.

Memories

His mind traveled over the years as Edmund, an octogenarian, sat back comfortably in his easy chair. Voyages into his memories always created so many wonderful emotions, brought smiles, and thoughts of old and valued friends.

There was Milton, one of his best friends. He was one of the boys, age 12, in his Boy Scout troop, his tent mate in Boy Scout camp, his roommate in college and the best man in his wedding. They had kept in touch over the many years though their professions caused them to live far apart.

Edmund recalled the song which the two of them sang so often sitting around the campfire at Boy Scout camp at night. He paraphrased the original version which helped to guide his life and now is a metaphor which reflects the winter of his life.

"Softly falls the light of day,
As my campfire fades away.
Silently I have to ask,
Have I done my daily task?
Have I kept my honor bright?
Can I guiltless sleep tonight?
Have I done and have I dared,
Everything to be prepared.

Quietly we soon must part,
Pledging ever in my heart,
Striving to do my best each day,

As I travel the rest of the way.
Happiness I'll try to give,
Still trying a better life to live.
'Till all the world is joined in love,
Living in peace under skies above."

Emotions overcame him. He wished that he could capture this friendships and so many other wonderful memories and feelings on paper …..and then fell peacefully asleep.

In My World

"Grandma, tell me about what it was like when you were little," asked 10-year-old Claire.

"It was really quite different," answered grandma. "In my world we had no television, no cell phones, we had no iPods, couldn't send text messages, no computers, and no McDonald's and many of us did not have cars."

"Oh my gosh, grandma, you must have been bored to tears, and where did you go out to eat? " replied Claire in awe.

"No, honey, we had a wonderful time in my world. We played outside together much of the time. We would play hopscotch on the sidewalk with our friends, celebrate birthdays with our friends, play games together, do our homework together, tell scary stories, and really had fun together. We all ate together at the kitchen table at home and shared what was new or different each day, laughed together, and discussed some of the happenings in our community and in our world with our parents. Going out to eat was usually at a restaurant and a very rare and special treat."

Claire looked puzzled. How could that be fun?

Grandma continued, "We didn't have air conditioning, dish-washers, clothes dryers, or microwave ovens. We all pitched in to help with clearing the tables, doing the dishes, and sometimes to hang clothes on the line outside to dry."

"Wow, grandma, I'm sure glad I didn't have to live in your world," quickly responded Claire.

"Honey it was a wonderful world. We had five and ten cent stores where you could actually buy things for five and ten cents. You could buy an ice cream cone and a Pepsi and ride on the streetcar for just a nickel.

During times of eating together, our parents taught us about good judgment and common sense, knowing the difference between right and wrong, and having to stand up and take responsibility for our own actions. We learned what a privilege it was to live in this great country of ours.

The words which we spoke in my world also had different meanings from what they mean today. For example, 'hardware' was something you found in the hardware store; 'software' wasn't even a word; 'chip' meant a piece of wood; 'pot' was something your mother cooked in, and 'grass' was mowed.

Claire, perhaps this explains why some people from my world find it difficult to deal with what we call the generation gap. It is good that some things have changed. But many valuable lessons learned in my world are being lost, and that bothers so many of us today."

A Variable Season

Winters do not vary much from year to year. Yes, some may be colder; some have more or less snow. Some aspects of winter however seem to have varied much more widely over my lifetime.

As a child winter was a wonderful and fun season. I couldn't wait to play in the snow, build snow men, go sledding, tube down hills, and have snowball fights with my friends. Winter's first snowflakes announced the coming of a fun time.

As a father of our young children winter still was a delightful time. Taking our children out to have fun in the snow was wonderful. Watching them learn to skate, ski, and to see the joy and hear the laughter as they fell off their sleds tumbling in the snow, fall on the ice rink then quickly get up to try again, all still warms my heart. Nothing in the winter blemished this pleasure.

As children matured, earning a living became my focus, wintertime pleasure shifted to enjoying the beauty of ice crusted trees sparkling in the sun and snow covered firs intensifying the blue of the sky. The time and effort required to shovel snow, clear ice covered walks, handle home maintenance problems caused by sub zero temperatures, drive to work on slippery roads and during snow storms however soon overruled the pleasures of winter.

Now being house bound leaves little to enjoy during winter. The focus must shift to other activities. The snowy scenes out the window are beautiful but in a very passive way.

How varied this season has become over the years.

How do People See Me?

"Wayne, I just came from a party for my son which was attended by people of all ages. People seemed friendly. Yet, I felt pretty much isolated. I sat at a table with seven other people I did not know. Several were middle aged couples, the others apparently their young children and one other octogenarian. At first the conversation was somewhat stilted as we did not seem to have anything in common.

Finally one of the younger fellows leaned over and asked how I know the fellow at the next table who is throwing this party.

"He is my son," I answered.

"Wow, you look young enough to be his brother," was the response. Not knowing that I heard her, one of the women across the table said to the man next to her, "In fact the old geezer looks like he is on his last legs."

That started me thinking about how do people see not only me but all "golden agers."

His 90 year old friend Wayne who could be quite blunt replied, "That was a terrible thing for that bitch to say, Larry. I would have told her that she will not be invited to my funeral."

"My son would have scalped me, Wayne. But think about it, have you ever wondered how people see you?"

"You know what, Larry, I don't give a damn what they think. I'm 90 years old and can say what I want." A moment of silence. Wayne seemed to be thinking it over.

"Wayne, I am not talking about how people think about us oldsters personally but how our generation is viewed by younger people. Like so many other elderly people I am still active, as you know. My ability to grasp issues, intuitiveness, ability to organize, discern the core, go to the heart of a problem, identify and prioritize the necessary action my insight and sixth sense and inner drive to get things done, is still very much intact.

My ability to understand some newspersons who speak too fast, and people who do not face me when they speak, has diminished despite newfangled hearing aids, and I cannot work or move as fast as I did in my youth. My mind still pushes me faster than my body can move. My mind says go and my body says whoa. I also find that I sleep less and need naps during the day."

"Yep, Larry, I guess that how we are viewed depends which side of us others see. Do they see our abilities or our disabilities? You know that applies to handicapped persons of all ages. Disadvantaged people still have a lot of abilities."

"Boy, you are as sharp as ever, Wayne. Indeed people with disadvantages have a lot of assets. As I see it however, there is one difference between us and the disabilities which younger people encounter. Once the abilities of the younger group are identified, and many agencies perform this task, it is easier to find a self supporting position for them. In our case, no one is interested in searching for our experience, wisdom and strengths. In this fast moving world the energy to maintain a rapid pace is a most important asset. We have to find the niche which is satisfying and which we can be pursue at our pace, or else life gets boring and or self image is diminished. I agree with you. How others see us can create how we are treated by them."

Stressful Suspension

Since my husband died I had felt quite alone
To depression I often felt very much prone.
My children urged that I travel again
To finally break this loneliness chain.

To drive out West I then planned a trip
To refresh my spirit and to come to grip
The past was great but there's a future to face
If a quality of life I am again to embrace.

I stopped at a diner along the way
To freshen up and my hunger to fray'
Then I noticed a man across the aisle.
He looked up at me and began to smile.

His brow then furrowed, he seemed to search
For something on which he could not perch.
Alone at the table he returned to his meal,
And shook his head, like it couldn't be real.

Who is that man at the table across the aisle?
He has such a familiar and pleasant smile.
The waitress smiled as she served him his meal
Why does he have such apparent appeal?

Have I met him before, I just can't recall
The man with white hair and quite tall.
Then it came to me, but it couldn't be.
My minds must be playing tricks on me.

Our eyes met again which caused him to rise,
Though he seemed to question if this is wise,
And came to my table and humbly asked,
"You look so familiar, a memory of the past?

Forgive me for asking, I am usually not brash,
But the impossible came as an improbable flash.
I know it is rude to interrupt while you are eating
But do you happen to be Elizabeth Keating?"

"Then you are Brock Thorp, my beau at College
Whose football stardom was aptly acknowledged."
I responded delighted, with a pounding heart.
"I recall how hard it was for us to part."

"You were the homecoming queen admired by all
Our breaking up, to me, was a heartbreaking fall.
But why do you travel apparently alone,?"
He quietly continued in a respectful tone.

"My husband died two years ago," I said
"And I'm trying to restore a new life ahead.
And you too are apparently on your own.
I noticed that you were eating quite alone."

"My wife Mary after years of despair
Passed away peacefully. She left us one heir.
I have no destination as I travel west.
There's only one stop I must make on my quest.

My grandson who lives in Rockaway Beach
Is the one destination which I must reach.

His wedding is still one week away
So some sightseeing is possible along the way.

What about you, what are your travel plans?"
"To enjoy the sights, I have time on my hands."
"Can we caravan west? I don't want to be rash
It would be delightful old memories to rehash."

I thought for a moment and then replied,
"It should add much pleasure to the ride,
To share the course of our lives, but within limitations
And I won't intrude on your grandson's occasion."

"I know he would be happy to meet the person
Upon whom, heartbreak and all, I have cast no aspersion.
I know he will like you and you will like him
And when I say this, it's not just on a whim."

My mind is in turmoil, this is moving too fast.
"Let's just travel and enjoy the scenery vast.
There are many memories I must still diffuse,
The loss of my husband left a very deep bruise."

Our relaxed drive west was delightful and heady
But for a deeper relationship I still was not ready.
We decided to stay in touch, to see each other again
That road side meeting surely wasn't in vain.

Imagine a stop for lunch at an Inn
Which could cause such turmoil from within
Filled with promise but with nagging apprehension
To put one's life into such stressful suspension.

Roles I've have played

It never occurred to me that I have played various roles in my life. Looking back, I realize many indeed have been played. Only one has been an acting role, that of the butler in "Charley's Aunt', the senior high school play.

There has been no training for the many real life roles into which I have been cast; the only child, the refugee, the football player, the soldier, the college student, the husband, the wage earner, the father, the grandfather, the volunteer, and now the great grandfather. What a cast of characters! Each role necessitated on the job training, each survived a learning period with accompanying mistakes and successes, each with its joys and it tears.

Each role was accompanied by an adjustment period, some longer, some shorter, some still in progress. It is said that there is never time to do it right, but always time to do it over. Unfortunately that does not apply to the roles which we encounter in life. One should do it right the first time.

Since that is not possible, I have found that there is another role which helps, the role of humor. It sure helps to smooth the bumps in the road for those who are impacted by my inexperience. I must remember that those who have become a member of the cast in my life's drama also have to navigate through on the job training and adjustment time.

A reporter visited Kuwait several years before the Gulf War and noted that it was the role of the women to walk ten feet behind their husbands as a sign of respect for his authority. She returned to

Kuwait recently and observed that women now walk several yards ahead of their husbands. Quite an apparent adjustment in the role each played. She approached one of the women for an explanation.

"This is marvelous," said the journalist. "What has caused this progress for women?"

Responded the Kuwaiti woman, "Land mines."

Special Meaning

In late February 2003 I received a call from my grandson Bryan who was attending the Officer Training School at Maxwell Air Force Base in Montgomery, Alabama. "Granddad, I am graduating on March 4 and would be proud if you could come here to pin on my lieutenant's bar at the graduating ceremony."

I still feel how deeply I was touched. Naturally, my wife and I flew to Montgomery. It was a great and confidence building experience. Our country is in great hands with these young leaders. My heart beat as I proudly pinned the bars on my grandson at the commissioning ceremony. Before leaving Montgomery I gave Bryan the Bronze Stars I was awarded for heroism during WWII.

Bryan's tours of duty included Qatar and Iraq, then work on guidance systems for satellite weapons to track and destroy satellite missiles aimed at the US by unfriendly forces. His degree from the University of Minnesota was in Aeronautical Engineering. He has received promotions over the years from second lieutenant, to first lieutenant to captain with significant responsibility increases and achievement awards.

Bryan visited us a few weeks ago and brought me his major's insignia, the rank to which he had just been promoted. He and his family will be moving to Washington, DC from Denver in August for an 18 month assignment either as the Air Force aide to a Senator or to the White House as the Air Force military attaché.

I have many items which have special meaning. But this one I keep on my desk. It is from a special grandson who is devoting is life to the service of our country. It touches me very deeply.

The Inanimate Walls

Yes, we do hang pictures on walls but it is the pictures, not the walls which draw our attention. Walls only define the living spaces and thus do not influence my life at all.

Walls took on an entire and intruding character when we moved into a condo. Suddenly they made me very much aware of them. They required many turns through narrower hallways to access the living spaces.

They became even more confining as I graduated from cane to walker to electric scooter. As a matter of fact, they became quite aggressive as I first tried to navigate the scooter around sharp corners and through the narrower hallways. The bruises on my arms testified to their aggressiveness. My scooter, not having had anger management training, responded by scraping and gauging walls, corners and doors.

I soon had to teach it to settle down. The handyman to make the repairs enjoyed the work and income but the frequent repairs became too costly.

Strange how these inert walls then changed again; they became my friends. They provide me with support as I transfer from scooter to other facilities to which scooter access is not possible. No more confrontations!

Hmm.... I certainly have not changed so it is evident that the inanimate walls have.

The Mother-in-Law

"Paul, I recently met some people who remembered your mother-in-law. They spoke very highly of her."

"She was a wonderful person, Jim. You know they say that one marries only the person he/she loves, not the spouse's whole family. This is not always true. I became a part of my wife's family.

My mother-in-law became a favorite from the very beginning. I learned later that while I dated her daughter she advised her not to let this one get away. This confidence after the mother of the first girl I dated forbade her daughter to see me anymore as I had no upward mobility."

"What was it that made you feel comfortable with her?"

"Her courage, the love she had for her four children which she raised after the early passing of her husband; how hard she worked to support them with the meager wages she received; the value she placed on maintaining contact with her extended family; how she always saw the good side of even the direst situation, and yes, her quirky humor as well."

"Quirky humor, Paul?"

"We still laugh often at the things she would do. She experienced many aches and pains and had to be urged repeatedly to see a doctor. When she finally yielded and returned from her visit we would ask if she told him about one or more ailments from which we knew she suffered.

Her answer, "No, he's the doctor, let him find out.""

"We always had tea and some of the delicious cookies she baked when we visited. She would always add three or more teaspoons of sugar to her tea."

"Isn't that too sweet for you?" we would ask.

"Oh no," she would reply. "I don't stir it."

"She loved to have everyone come to her small house for dinner and family occasions. There was always room at the table and no one minded sitting jammed against their neighbor.

How well I remember the many grandchildren and the cousins, sitting on the living room floor at her home singing together accompanied by a guitar strummed by one of the grandchildren, the adults sitting in a circle around them. A family united in warmth and in spirit.

These were precious moments and memories she created which will long be remembered by us all.

There are not many like her."

The Old Grouch

During a sleepless and painful night, and the few minutes of interrupted sleep, he had dreamt he was an old car. He was being hauled to the scrap yard because he has bumps and dents and scratches in his finish and his paint job is getting a little dull. But that's not the worst of it. His headlights were out of focus making it hard to see things up close. His traction was not as graceful as it once was. He slipped and slid and skidded and bumped into things even in the best of weather. He held up traffic and people were shouting at him to get out of the way.

Waking up in the morning, he was ready to bite anyone who did not tiptoe around him.

She burst into the room with an exuberant, "Good Morning" which startled all of us. It was as though her trumpet blare announced that she had just won the mega lottery. The jolt of her loud and high energy loosened what little restraint he had.

He shouted, "Just sit down and eat your breakfast."

"My, what a grouch we have at the table this morning," she responded. "Have you had rabies shot recently?"

His face reddened in anger and he slammed his fist on the table. Unfortunately he hit the plate in front of him sending it shattering on the tile kitchen floor. His son rushed to move the two grandchildren further from their grandfather and his daughter-in-law ran to get the broom and dust pan to clean up the broken china. A long and uncomfortable silence blanketed all.

Suddenly he heard a voice say, "Wake up, grandpa! You must have had an awful dream. It's time to come to the table for breakfast." As he struggled into his robe he heard his granddaughter repeat what his wife often told him:

"No matter how grouchy you're feeling,
You'll find a smile more or less healing.
It grows in a wreath all around the front teeth
Thus preserves the face from congealing."

The Perfect Day

Aches and pains are constant companions but lo and behold I awoke this morning pain-free after five hours of uninterrupted sleep, a first for many years. The sun was shining and the birds were singing and a great breakfast awaited me.

Now there was a decision to be made. What should I do first? Should I finished preparing my tax return, answer several e-mails, send out birthday cards, one already overdue, do the filing to unclutter my desk, read the morning's newspaper, follow up on an insurance problem or balance my checkbook?

They say that it is difficult to make a decision if the pros and cons fall into the gray area. It's not tough in this case. It's either black or white and this is clearly white. So I decided I would celebrate by taking a little nap first.

The next thing I know I am awakened for lunch. What should I do after lunch? Oh boy, there is a sweet 16 basketball game this afternoon. My alma mater's game is being televised. I decided to watch the game. Reclining in my chair was so comfortable that an entirely new program was on TV as I awoke. Well, I'll have to wait until we receive tomorrow's newspaper to learn how the game turned out. I'll put that on the list of things to do in the morning.

Now it's time for dinner. I enjoyed a great meal uninterrupted by telephone calls. I should certainly catch up on the news of the day. Now where did I put the newspaper? Unable to find it, I decided that the world will just have to take to take care of itself until morning. I'll put it on my list of things to do tomorrow.

By now it was bedtime again.
Now that's a perfect day.

The Reunion

I entered a garden with strangers many years ago
And planted seeds of friendship, some indeed did grow.
Some sprouted but distance intervened through the years.
They withered away, their seeds planted in other spheres.

I traveled back to the garden with hope to revive
Close friendships which may have somehow survived.
Others had returned with the same intent,
To recall the time together, a time well spent.

It was great to see old classmates again
All of us smiling through old age gathered pain.
Recalling the garden where we planted and enjoyed
Friendships, before jobs caused us to be deployed.

I found old friendships but again they were fleeting
No flowers emerged from this wonderful meeting.
But suddenly a flower arose from the old seeds planted
And a miracle of true friendship again I was granted.

From a Withered Tree a Flower Blooms

My trunk is peeling, the bark is loose
My branches wear very little green.
For many seasons I've withstood the abuse
But now I am beginning to lean.

Strong winds have begun to weaken the roots
Which have held me erect through the years.
Summer droughts and winter ice, apparently in cahoots,
Have eliminated so many of my treasured peers.

It's springtime, will I last this year?
Then I heard two men come up to me.
Is this the moment I have come to fear?
For a chainsaw in the hand of one I could see.

"This is the one I think we should get,"
Said the one as he started the saw.
"It's great firewood to store in my shed.
And it sure ain't against the law."

Then suddenly the other man shouted,
"Hold up, don't cut yet," he boomed.
"Come see the beauty it has sprouted".
There, attached to my roots, a flower had bloomed.

He turned off the saw and both of them stared,
And I was relieved and eternally grateful
For the bloom which this spring had bared
Had delayed an event quite fateful.

A Treasured Tree has Fallen

Carl and I were classmates at the University of Kansas in Chemical Engineering from our freshman year through graduate school. Our friendship deepened during this time. As luck would have it, we went to work in the same department for the same company in New Martinsville, West Virginia after graduating.

After four years Carl sought transfer to a location which offered more cultural venues than existed in the West Virginia town of 3000. After positions in New Jersey, then New York, he eventually ended up in Miami, Florida, where he bought and operated a flower shop.

We lost contact for a number of years. I held Carl in high respect. He was a very intelligent, tall, and handsome man who had a great voice, a sense of humor and was pleasant company. About 10 years ago I finally located Carl. He was caring for his male companion who had contacted Parkinson's disease. Carl felt isolated. I discovered that his hobby was writing poetry. Our friendship continued via frequent correspondence and phone calls ever since. We exchanged and commented on the poems we had written. He had no computer thus our written exchanges were by mail.

In June 2013 he left a message on our answering machine that I should not try to call him back. He would call again. He did not sound well. I waited four weeks and decided to call him. There was no response to many rings. After a few weeks I tried again with the same result.

I searched for his name in the Miami newspaper only to find, much to my sadness, that Carl had passed away in June. The poem

he sent after his last message in June was called '*Friends*'. It was
#178 of the 200 he had hoped to create.

'Friends are like a summer breeze.
Rustling through our family trees.
Not of our blood, nor of or genes,
They simply paint our lifetime scenes.

Gone from sight, but not from my mind,
They fill our lives with acts so kind,
That tears are shed when they are gone.
But certain sure, their deeds live on
Within our hearts and memories,
Still rustling through our family trees.'

A treasured tree had fallen.

Closure

"Closure" held no meaning for him. The sadness of losing a loved one cannot be shed any more than one can shed the darkness of night or the light of day. Very few days pass on which the memories of his beloved daughter do not burden his thoughts and drain his energy.

Beautiful, intelligent, talent, caring, poised, courageous, thoughtful, devoted mother, she became a role model for all who knew her. "Closure?" It just does not exist for him.

He had often tried to share his memories with her children when the families gathered for various occasions. The festive mood and the happy "catching up" with other family members at such events however made these a poor setting for reminiscing. They were so very young when she died. Now adults, they should know the legacy she left them and how very much she loved and cared for them to the very end. Why not write it down for them? The written word can be accessed and revisited forever.

Paper and pen in hand he began to let his memories flow, starting with her very early years.

As his mind drifted back to those years he smiled as he remembered her. She was not always such an angel at an early age. She had been a very strong willed and mischievous little girl. She had been particularly bad one day and her mother sent her to bed to take a nap. "If you force me to take a nap I will put this pearl in my nose," she threatened. Her mother warned her and finally threatened her if she did and WHAM, in went the pearl.

He remembered her watching television and kissing Dr. Kildare (Richard Chamberlain) on the TV set. He remembered her chasing chipmunks with a salt shaker during a trip to the Colorado Rockies because her grandfather had told her that is how you catch chipmunks. He remembered that when it became time to do the dinner dishes she would excuse herself to go to the bathroom and never make it back. He remembered her climbing out a window to 'run away" at age 11 for being 'sent to her room' for some infraction.

His thoughts, now translated to paper, raced through the years. Page after page described her character, her ability to recognize and face her own shortcomings, how insightful she was, how she left an enduring legacy of courage and strength for her children when she knew the end was near. He remembered the very happy moments with her, and why all she contacted admired and respected her.

He remembered one of the last moments with her. She had been diagnosed with breast cancer. For two years she underwent surgeries, chemotherapy and radiation therapy to fight this life threatening disease. She remained in control of the management of her treatments, never once complaining. She focused on educating and guiding her children toward a bright future and providing them with as much pleasure as possible. Her sincere smile continued to be her trademark throughout.

When all treatments failed she opted for a bone marrow transplant. He had held her hand as she laid in her hospital bed before being prepared for this procedure. She sensed his concern. "Dad," she said, "don't worry. I just need to go through this to get well." **She was consoling him**. Her courage, her positive outlook, her sensitivity, her intelligence, the breadth of her talents and interests, her drive for perfection, her integrity, and her love for her children have left such an enduring legacy.

Suppressing his tears he set all he had written aside to let the tsunami of emotions subside. His painful journey had taken his memories through the night into daylight. Slowly, in the solitude of his room, he began to realize what a gift she still is to him and to her children. Closure? No. But by letting his pen work through the deep sadness of the night he had reached the sunlight of the day to shine on him and her children forever. He smiled.

A Box of Tears

"Greg, we recently discussed how various important events in our lives are overwhelming and stressful because they are so numerous and concurrent. I recall telling you about sorting out the important one and placing the rest in a box so they can be opened at will, one at a time, on which to focus our energies with minimum distraction." said Jerry.

"I must now tell you of one box which refuses to stay locked. It is filled with tears. I can no longer control or influence the outcome, hard as I tried as the event was unfolding. Some say that if you once lock this box there is closure. The fact that the tears still reopen the box after so many years, to have even more tears added from time to time, refutes the word closure. It is the only event for which I have not achieved serenity and peace by placing it in a locked box."

"Jerry, I have thought a lot about our discussion and your most helpful and insightful comments. I see that you have also given it further thought. What caused you to notice that there is one locked box which cannot be kept closed?"

"Yesterday I was going through some photos and found a picture of our daughter Robin. She was 35 years old when she passed away over 23 years ago leaving three small children. Breast cancer had overcome her courageous year long fight during which she never lost focus on raising her beautiful children, remaining cheerful and forward looking until the last.

We had received a call from one of our daughters who was with her at the time to hurry up if we wanted to see Robin alive. We rushed to the hospital only to be met in a hall by two persons walking toward us from the hospital pastoral staff. By their walk I knew that Robin had passed away. To this day I vividly remember the loud throaty 'oh no' roar I involuntarily let out. It echoed down the hall as my knees buckled and I fell to the floor. The loss of our beloved daughter and the memory of that moment continue to open the box of tears.

Yet as more tears subside, the wonderful gift of the years she gave us, and the way her three children have matured, two became physicians and one is in graduate school studying in a related field. This allows me to close the box again, at least until the next time it springs open again."

I Feel No Fear

As I climbed the tree of life
Each branch different from the others
And reached the very top to see
The mountain ahead I had yet to scale
I did not fear, I did not fear.

If I could start over would I start the climb
Knowing the obstacles sure to come with time?
Of course I would, for the risks embolden
And each step should spur one's growth.
I should not fear, I should not fear.

The babbling brooks, the birds with their song,
The storms, the pains on the climb sure to come,
Will not deter my determination to continue ahead
To venture into the unknown so I started the trek.
I would not fear, I would not fear.

Bruised but still feisty I have reached the abyss
At the top of the mountain viewed from that tree.
From that ledge I gaze to see what lies ahead
Dense fog impedes the view; there is nothing I can see.
I still feel no fear, I still feel no fear.

If I could start over would I do it again?
I ask as I walk along the edge at the top.

Knowing eventually I must take the next step
Into the truly unknown from the top of this crest.
I do not fear, I do not fear.

We Come, We Experience, We Leave

We come into this life with nothing. My early experiences left me with no self confidence, locked into the lifestyle of the past, with fear of varying from tradition. The word creativity embodied disrespect and rebelliousness and was unheard of. That is who I was.

Once I saw and acknowledged that one's standing on an issue and lifestyle can be challenged and broadened, it became transformative.

I have learned that if one limits his actions to things with which nobody can find fault, one will not do much.

I have learned that one measures the size of accomplishments by the obstacles which had to be overcome.

I have learned that circumstances are beyond human control. My conduct however is very much in my power.

I have learned that a quiet, compassionate touch will calm pain and create warmth for the giver.

History is told through the voices of great men. It should also be told by those who live it. Yours and mine are such stories. Once I have told my story expansively, I have reclaimed my true identity.

We come into this life with nothing. We leave it with the incredible story of our lives.

The Four Seasons

Spring has arrived with all its appeal.
Trees stretch their limbs and flowers bloom
To paint a picture of beauty that's real
And the air is filled with a hint of perfume.

Summer then tries to nudge into place
As warm and humid air begins to appear'
Lightning, thunder and rain try to replace
The feeling of spring which we hold so dear.

A clear blue sky then embrace the trees
Flourishing green in glorious splendor,
And Summer's flowers sway in the breeze
Creating a feeling nothing else can engender.

Nature in the fall, with its mighty loom,
Weaves the leaves into a tapestry bright
A magnificent sight just outside my room
Bringing much of this season's delight.

Then softly winter spreads it blanket white
To protect all of the seasons displays
And footprints record all who travel across
The memories which always remain.

To my grandchildren I sometimes like to contend
That this applies to us humans as well.
As we travel life's seasons from beginning to the end
Each age has its beauty with a chance to excel.

As you weave the tapestry of the seasons ahead
Be aware of their beauty and carefully strive
To leave a legacy with each special thread
On which your descendents can thrive.

GERMANY

The Early Years

I was born in Schoenlanke, Germany, a typical small German village of 8,840 people. A market square at its center was dominated by the Evangelical church. A variety of stores and shops surrounded the large cobblestone square. Hirsekorn's Hotel was on one corner of this square.

Farmers brought their produce to this square on weekends and people from the area bought their week's requirements of fresh vegetables, eggs and other farm products. It was the event of the week. Hirsekorn's Hotel was a popular "watering hole," restaurant, and source of fresh meat and poultry.

Grandmother and I shared a small rectangular bedroom which had one window facing a corner of the market square. My parents had the adjoining bedroom with a view overlooking a large, glass-roofed veranda. It was from the large bedroom window overlooking the veranda through which I later saw a most frightening scene.

Vivid memories come back about a large square brick stove located in the center of the large kitchen. A heavy metal plate covered the top of the brick enclosure. The plate contained several large round openings into which successively smaller and removable concentric metal rings fit. These could be removed to accommodate various sized pots and pans. Compartments on the sides of the brick stove were used to keep meals warm and to bake. Wood and coal provided the heat. What a wonderful invention. My mother and grandmother did all of the cooking and baking for the restaurant, for hotel guests and for us.

Mother and grandmother also cleaned and made up the hotel rooms and did the laundry. The laundry and the meat processing facilities were on one side of our enclosed rectangular courtyard one level below the kitchen level. All laundry, as well as wood, coal, water, and meats had to be carried up from the courtyard to the kitchen, living quarters, hotel and butcher shop levels. 112

A hand operated water pump, the source of all our water needs those early years, was located adjacent to the laundry room.

Prior to the advent of indoor plumbing, family and guests had to go down the stairs, across the open cobblestone yard to use the outhouse (a four holer, two for men and two for women). I can well remember how scared I was (and cold in the winter) to go across the courtyard after dark to use these "wooden benches" with holes much too large for me. Was I going to fall in? I could hear the occasional movement of the cattle in the adjacent cattle barn, which further stirred the imagination of a three year old.

Food was cooled from ice brought in from a huge ice pit. During the winter my father, with helpers, would go to the frozen nearby lake to saw and remove large cubes of ice weighing 50 to 80 pounds each. The blocks were hauled back to the ice storage pit located at the courtyard level adjacent to the wine cellar entrance. Ice blocks were placed on the floor of the pit. Each succeeding layer was covered with sawdust for insulation to keep them from freezing together again. Many tons of ice were stored in layers up to 20 feet high, enough to last until the following winter.

Transportation was with horse and buggy. My father eventually acquired the first automobile in the village. The top speed of this automobile was 20 miles per hour. What a magnet for me. One day I got into the car and pretending to drive it I accidentally loosened the brake. The car started to roll backward.

It rolled out the open, huge wooden gate. I panicked as the car backed into the street, ramming against the wall of the building across the way. Fortunately no one was hurt nor was the car or the building damaged.

My father gave me a severe spanking, followed by being locked in a small dark closet, that I dreamt of rolling uncontrollably backward for years thereafter.

I was expected to learn and carry on my father's trade. Six generations of Hirsekorns were butchers. My future was ordained by family tradition.

Father was a volunteer fireman and would respond to local fires.

We were in a restaurant during a visit to Charnikau (now Czarnkow, Poland), a village about 14 miles away, when lightning hit a nearby church. I was about five years old at the time. My father, along with the others in the restaurant rushed out of the restaurant to fight the fire at the church. I was left there alone. Another lightning bolt struck the restaurant and the room filled with smoke. I panicked. Eventually word reached my father who returned to get me out after he realized he had left me there. It took many years to overcome my fear of thunderstorms.

All showed unquestioning respect for authority. No one questioned or spoke back to parents, teachers, rabbis, ministers, local mailmen, provincial or national officials. Men in uniform were especially respected. The constant battles between my parents, painful to me, never being able to please my father and his hair trigger temper made me lose self confidence. I had a very poor self image at this stage of my life. I tried to avoid verbal confrontations, was easily intimidated and responded to orders quickly and without questioning.

Then in January 1933, at age 8, my whole world suddenly turned even worse. But that is another story.

The Gathering Storm

Hitler was well organized prior to becoming Chancellor of Germany. The *Sturm Abteilung,* SA, (Storm Troops) had been formed years prior to 1933. These were the misfits who would use beatings and murder if necessary to intimidate any opposition. Hitler dressed them in fancy brown uniforms and let it be known that they were the power and future of Germany. They paraded through towns with stirring martial band music, goose stepping with flags flying! Adults were stirred by these thrilling spectacles of rejuvenating German power and the future it promised. Kids loved the parades and followed the marchers with enthusiasm.

Ernst Rohm, leader of the SA, stated that, "Brutality is respected. The people need wholesome fear. We will make them shatteringly submissive." SA membership soon outnumbered the police. They became an increasingly intimidating force. (Hitler later had Rohm, who helped put Hitler in power, and the next level of SA leadership killed one night {code named 'Night of The Long Knifes'} because Rohm had become too powerful. The SA was put under the control of Hitler's SS {Schutzstaffel – Protections Squad} which Hitler controlled.)

We felt the effect of the Nazi regime only a few weeks after the end of January 1933. Our street was blocked off and the SA broke into our hotel and living quarters, "to search for communists." Two of their sort were dressed up as "communists" and were placed on the roof of our hotel. The police, outnumbered and intimidated, said this was perfectly legal. It was an exercise to protect the German people. Nazi leaders soon organized a nationwide boycott of Jewish businesses on April 1, 1933. It lasted only one day as the boycott affected the entire German economy.

The *Evangelische* School I attended along with the other Jewish children was renamed the "Adolph Hitler" school on May 18, 1933 and all Jewish children were expelled. The Catholic school eventually accepted us.

The Nazis soon began to pressure Catholic teachers and students to join the Nazi party. Our lives in the Catholic school soon became difficult. Non-Jewish friends, soccer team mates and school mates, began to avoid me after they joined the Hitler Youth. They were taught to hate Jews. They took great pride being a Nazi, wearing the flashy Nazi uniform, marching in parades and participating in bonfires with the SA. Teacher who may have been neutral or even friendly to Jewish children were unable to stop class mates from the harassing us.

School books soon began to contain anti-Semitic lessons. Compulsory classes in "Race Hygiene" were taught in elementary Schools. Small children liked the glamour of the uniform and they too were taught to hate Jews.

I was often the target for beatings. One day a Jewish class mate, Martin Moses, came running to my mother who was cooking in the kitchen to tell her that many kids had trapped me and were beating me bloody. She ran out of our house, still wearing her apron, to rescue me.

Horrible and degrading cartoons about Jews soon began to appear on the street kiosks. These are the cylindrical structures at many street corners on which advertising was posted. Can you imagine how it felt seeing such cartoons as I ventured outside to play or cringed to go to school?

All other political parties were banned in July 1933. Music by Jewish composers like Mendelssohn & Mahler was also banned as was Jazz and swing music. The Nazis believed the later to be of Negro origin.

Raids and break-ins by the S.A. into our home and business increased in frequency over the years. Calls to the police brought the response that they were not aware of any illegal activity in our neighborhood. One of my father's old army friends who participated in these raids waited until after midnight to sneak into the hotel to tell my father that he really did not want to do this. He had to participate in order not to lose his job.

One day the SA forced us all into the billiard room and lined us up against the wall on which a huge mirror and glass shelves holding glasses was mounted. They pulled their pistols and shot into the mirror behind us warning us that this will happen to all Jews soon.

Jewish customers continued to patronize our hotel restaurant and butcher shop. All non-Jewish help resigned. A rare dance was held in the ballroom one evening. Since this was an all Jewish affair, the doors to the hotel were locked. A rush of footsteps outside the hotel warned my parents to lock me into their bedroom as the front door was broken down by the SS. The Nazis stormed onto the dance floor hitting the panicked crowd with their heavy brass belt buckles. The only escape was through windows facing the cobblestoned Bromberger Strasse one floor below. Several experienced injuries from the fall. I watched this through the large window in my parent's bedroom overlooking the glass domed veranda.

What I saw next really frightened me. An SS man had raised his pistol to my father's chest saying, "I think I'll shoot you." My mother stepped between the gun and my father and said, "If you do, you will have to shoot him through me." I still recall the terror I felt and can imagine the fright my parents must have felt at that moment.

A horse drawn wagon with a post mounted in the center appeared as I looked out of the window one afternoon. A nude man and woman were tied to this pole. The sign on the wagon read, "This is how the Jews are polluting our Aryan Race." I later learned that one of the two was Jewish, the other a non-Jew. Public embarrassment for such relationships took other forms in other locations. We began to hear hushed voices relating how some people had just 'disappeared."

My father continued to believe that all of this madness would soon pass and Germany would return to normal. We would not be touched because of his military service, for which he was awarded two Iron Crosses. "See, they did not shoot me," was his response.

The Nazi regime was uncertain at the time about how to implement the "Final Solution," the elimination of all Jews from Germany. Should Jews be frightened out of the country, deported or murdered. Their "problem" was that almost no other country would accept the German Jews. This eventually led them to decide that murder was the only "practical" solution.

An old and credible friend of my father's snuck into the hotel one night and warned him that we could all soon be arrested. This finally triggered my father's response to reset our sails.

The circumstances which saved us from the 'final solution' is another story.

The Survivors Miracles

How were we able to survive 'The Final Solution' when so many millions were systematically murdered by the Nazis? It was a series of events, sacrifice and courage, which converged.

My father wrote to Alex Rieger who had visited Schoenlanke with his son Jack in 1922. The Rieger family lived in Kansas City and Alex Rieger had become the American Consular to Czechoslovakia. He had married my grandmother's sister. She had immigrated to the USA many years prior.

"Could you arrange to get us a Visa to immigrate to Argentina?" he wrote. Argentina offered free land to any immigrants who would develop land in its interior. My father felt that if we had land we would be able to raise enough food to feed the family. All other countries known to us, including the United States, severely restricted Jewish immigration. It was unlikely we would be accepted anywhere else.

"You will come to the United States and I will arrange to get you on the immigration quota." was Alex's reply. Call it fate, good luck, or the goodness of the power above, Rieger's 1922 visit and the February and August 1936 Olympics to be held in Germany combined to save our lives. We were placed on the US immigration quota on January 23, 1936 thanks to the efforts of Alex Rieger. He also guaranteed that we would not become a burden to the US welfare program.

The 1936 Olympics delayed implementing the Nazis extermination " final solution." The winter Olympics were to open in

February 1936 at Garmisch-Partenkirchen. This was to be followed by the 1936 summer Olympics in Berlin. Hitler and his henchmen realized that world media would be reporting on events in Germany and the whole world would be watching. They would have to sanitize the country of its hateful persecution before visitors and the media appeared on the scene. Orders went out to remove all visible traces of anti-Semitism. The posters and signs disappeared from the kiosks and the press was ordered to tone down the virulent and dehumanizing attacks on Jews. This was not the image of Germany they wanted the world to see. Some barriers were lowered for those who may wish to leave. A sum of $25/person and one suitcase per person could be taken out of the country. Items of value, such as gold and jewelry, could not be included with the personal possessions.

The decision to abandon all that had been built by 5 generations of Hirsekorns and to start all over in a distant land where the language and the culture were unknown with such meager resources took a great deal of courage. The hotel, living quarters, restaurant and wine cellars, meat processing facilities, butcher shop, smoke house, sausage production equipment, laundry room, farms, wagons and car, and all of the contents were abandoned. Cash and other valuables were given to my father's brother, my uncle George Hirsekorn living in Berlin.

My father was 39 years old at the time. How would he be able to take care of his family? My mother, also 39 years old, would be leaving her brothers and their families behind, not knowing if they would ever see them again. (Over eighty of her brothers, their wives and children were murdered by the Nazis in concentration camps.)

The physical and emotional stress for my parents and for my 72 year old grandmother must have been overwhelming.

I was immediately sent to my uncle in Berlin. Jews were not as easily identified in Berlin as they were in small towns like Schoenlanke. Also the 1936 Olympics had toned down the extreme persecution and dehumanizing of Jews. My parents did not accompany me as they were not sure that they could leave before being arrested. They also needed time to try to decide what limited items they could stuff into one suitcase for each of us and one steamer trunk to take along and survive in this country so unknown to us.

My parents come to Berlin on March 9, 1936. On March 10, 1936 we took the train to Paris after tear filled goodbyes. Another train took us to Cherbourg to board the ship Berengaria for New York. We later learned that the Gestapo had come to arrest my parents the day after they left for Berlin.

It was the merging of Alex Rieger's 1922 visit, his connections and good will, the easing of restrictions caused by the 1936 Olympics and above all my father's and mother's courage which produced the miracle of our survival to the blessings of the USA.

Everyone Will Understand You

A man named Ziggi Casper was a character who frequented my father's restaurant in Germany in the early 1930's. He would say "mixed pickle water closet" whenever he lost a hand playing cards. "What does this mean?" I eventually asked my father. Not knowing either he brushed me aside with, "It means toilet." This knowledge would have consequences years later.

Not sure we could flee from Germany in time, my parents had sent me to Berlin in 1936. They promised that they and my grandmother would join me there shortly.

I decided that I need to learn how to speak English before departing to America where only English is spoken. Fortunately an American taught English not too far from where I lived with uncle George, my father's brother.

The teacher rattled on incessantly in a language I did not understand. Finally he said to me in German, "Would you really like to learn how to speak English so that everyone in America will understand you?" he asked.

"Yes sir," I replied with enthusiasm.

"You will need to learn only three words and everyone in America will understand you." Wow, this will be easier than I thought.

"But you must pronounce each word clearly." I promised to pronounce every word clearly!

"The first word is *kiss*," he said. "kuss," I responded. "No, no. no. That is German.

Repeat after me slowly, *kiss.*" I worked hard to pronounce it correctly and finally got it.

"The next word is *my*. Say it.""Mein," I said."Wrong again! Don't press your tongue to your mouth after you say *mei,*" he replied.

Well, I worked hard until it led to the last word. I could hardly wait. What a wonderful language!

Now the last word, *"Ass"* he continued. I learned how to pronounce all three perfectly.

A distant relative, Jack, who spoke some German, met us at the port in New York after sailing across the ocean with my parents and grandmother. He had reserved sleeping compartments for our trip to Kansas City, his home. This was like living in a fairy tale.

We went to the dining car once were settled. Wow, how beautiful! Upholstered chairs, linen covered tables set with fine china plates, crystal goblets and real silverware, and real flowers greeted us. It was a little intimidating to me. I must be on my very best behavior.

The swaying motion of the train soon began to arouse the motion sickness I experienced at sea. I lost my appetite!

A waiter dressed in a white shirt, bow tie, and black vest, with a white towel neatly draped over his arm, placed a silver plate containing many ugly black, shiny, neatly piled oval nuggets on our table. I had never seen such things before.

"What are these?" I asked Jack. "They are olives," he replied. "Everyone in America eats them. Take one." My father gave me look which told me I had better do what Jack said. I reluctantly bit into one and immediately my stomach began to fight back.

Not wanting to get sick in that elegant dining room, I rushed into the aisle in the adjoining sleeping car desperately looking for a toilet. A tall black man wearing a black uniform with brass buttons and a red cap came toward me in the narrow passage way. Desperately searching for the word for toilet I recalled what Ziggi Casper had said in our restaurant many years ago.

"Wo ist das mixed pickle water closet?" I asked him urgently. He gave me puzzled look. I knew I could not last much longer I repeated it again, "Wo ist das mixed pickle water closet?" He merely shook his head.

Finally I remembered the words I was taught only weeks before which would make everyone in America understand me.

"Kiss my ass," I said. The porter picked me up by my lapel and I threw up all over him.

Obviously the poor man did not understand English.

W W II

Getting into the War

I wanted to get into the war against the Nazis after America declared war on December 7, 1941. I was too young (17) to be accepted into the service. In 1942 the Navy had started to train pilots to fly off aircraft carriers called the V-12 program. I decided this was the quickest way for me to get into the battle.

I passed the written intelligence tests and appeared for the physical exam shortly thereafter. Numbers were painted on the chests of the volunteers in the order in which they arrived for the physical. I was number 1, the first to arrive that morning. I was jubilant to hear that I passed the physical and was to appear the next day to be sworn in. Several Navy officers came into the room as I was getting dressed. They called for Number 1. They were very angry.

"Are you trying to sabotage the Navy?" I had no idea what they were talking about.

"No Sir." I answered.

"How long have you been a citizen of the United States?" they asked.

"Almost a whole year." I responded.

"Don't you know that you have to be a citizen for 10 years before you can become an officer in the navy?" they yelled. "Get the hell out of here before we have you arrested."

I was crushed! It took me several days to get over this blow. Entering the war would have to wait until I was drafted. (The navy dropped the 10-year citizenship requirement as the war progressed. Most military services eventually began to grant US citizenship to those serving in the military even before the 5-year US residency requirement was satisfied.) A term at Kansas City Junior College followed. I was drafted by the Army in December 1942.

Early Training

We arrived at the Fort Leavenworth Kansas Induction Center at about 2:00 A.M. on an icy cold morning in January 1943 and were marched from barracks to barracks in search of available empty bunks. I was cold and physically exhausted by the time a place was found for me at 2:45 A.M. It had been a long day and an emotional one at home.

We were awakened at 4:30 A.M. and marched to a large hall after less than two hours of sleep and given a written test. It turned out to be an IQ test, the results of which, unknown to me, would have far reaching consequences.

Six months intensive basic training in the 20th Armored Division being formed at Camp Campbell, Kentucky (now Fort Campbell) followed. Training included physical conditioning, learning to march and take orders, firing various weapons, disassembling them, naming all the parts, and putting them back together in a hurry, driving tanks, crawling under barbed wire while machine guns fired live ammunition over our heads as simulated mines exploded around us, map reading, enemy and friendly tank and aircraft recognition. My Scouting experiences sure helped.

Camp Campbell was the only place I had ever lived where the milk tasted like onions. Cattle fed on wild onions which grew on the ranges where they grazed. It was also the only place where one could be in red mud up to one's ankles after a rain and still have dust blow in one's face.

As basic training came to an end, I was advised by my company commander that my IQ qualified me to take a test to enter a new army program. He asked that I take the test. This turned out to be for the ASTP, Army Specialized Training Program, designed to provide badly needed trained engineers, chemists and other technical personnel. ASTP was an accelerated college level program designed to fill this need as quickly as possible. I had reached the rank of PFC, Private First Class, which I had to give up as no one in ASTP had any rank.

I passed the test and was sent to join a unit at Ohio State University in Columbus, Ohio. My chemistry and physics grades were more than adequate. I was thus placed in the second "year" of the accelerated program. The problem was that mathematics at this level started with calculus.

I had almost flunked algebra in high school and thus had also avoided trigonometry, both prerequisites for calculus. It was sink or swim. If I got less than a "C" in any course, I would flunk out of ASTP.

Fortunately I had two great and intelligent roommates; Nick George, whose home was Louisville, Kentucky, and Don Reaugh, from Newton, Kansas. They were willing to help me even thought they were very busy trying to keep up with their own work. We became good friends.

I really worked hard and wished I had not let my attitude toward a high school teacher affect my learning algebra. My grades in all other subjects were good and I eventually made a "C" in calculus, thanks mostly to their help.

The Idiots Won the War

Learning how to drive a tank was a trying experience. Fifteen of us were marched to a line of fifteen Sherman M-4 medium tanks one afternoon at Camp Campbell, KY, basic training with the newly formed 20th Armored Division. The order came to get into the driver's seat on the left side of one of the tanks. An instructor, fresh off a Kentucky farm, sat in the assistant driver's (bow gunner's) seat.

"OK, start the motor," the instructor said. I had no idea how to start the motor. The control panel to my left was entirely strange to me.

"Start the engine," he repeated.

"I don't know how to do that," I pleaded sheepishly.

"You start it with the magnetos," he responded. I had no idea what a magneto was.

"Dummy, you squeeze them bottom two toggle switches together and then push the top toggle switch to the right." I did that and the tank jerked and I killed the engines. The tanks ahead of me started to move.

"What kind of dummies are they drafting nowadays? You're holding up the parade!" he shouted. "Put the clutch in before starting the engine!"

I finally got it started but there was no steering wheel, just a couple of steel bars with hand grips coming up from the floor of the tank.

I asked, "How do I steer this thing?"

"Ain't you never driven a tractor before?"

"No sir." I responded.

Well, you've certainly driven a truck."

"No sir,' I said intimidated.

"You've sure driven a car before, ain't you?" he said in disbelief.

"I was just starting to learn, sir"

"We ain't never going to win no war with idiots like you." was his angry reply. "Have you learned how to ride a bicycle?"

"Yes sir."

"Well thank God for that. Pull that there left lever to turn left and the right one to turn right, just like on the bicycle." The tanks were moving forward and I was still sitting there holding up the rest.

"Let's get going, jerk. I ain't got all day to sit here with you. And don't forget to double clutch when shifting down," he ordered.

Oh my God, what is "double clutch?" What is shifting down? Do I dare ask when the pressure is on to move forward and this intimidating guy has no patience with me. I put the tank in gear and started moving forward, my tank staggering from side to side like a drunk, doing the tango down the road. Moving 34 tons of steel was scary! But now how do you stop this beast with no brakes?

I eventually learned how to drive a tank, to "double clutch", how to stop the monster and how to back it up.

And needless to say, over more than 11 million of us idiots won the war.

Heading Overseas - Discordant

The ASTP program was discontinued after six months. The need for front line soldiers was greater than the need for technical personnel. We were quickly reassigned to combat units. Nick George, Don Reaugh, and I were assigned to the 14th Armored Division which had just returned from maneuvers in Louisiana. The division was at Camp Campbell, Kentucky, preparing to head overseas in two weeks. Nick went to the 62nd Armored Infantry Battalion, Don to the 19th Armored Infantry Battalion and I to "C" company of the 25th Tank Battalion.

The soldiers in the 14th Armored Division were recruited from the farm lands and hills of Kentucky and Tennessee. Only six of us in "C" company, reassigned from the ASTP program, had any college education. We were pretty much outcasts in the company. The others resented college students.

It was also the first time I encountered overt anti-Semitism in the army. One of the fellows in the company said that the only reason he joined the army was to learn how to kill Jews, and that Jews never get into combat units. They always get the soft rear echelon jobs. Several of the others agreed until I spoke up and told him to start with me as I was Jewish. He said that I must have been an oversight. I mentioned that there were six in our company of 150 men who were of the Jewish faith. This makes it 4% Jewish while the Jewish population in the US was 1.7%. This was a total commitment to stop Hitler. He backed off so that no fight developed.

Anti-Semitism and disdain for "college boys" disappeared only after we entered combat.

Our port of debarkation was New York.

First Combat

Our first combat assignment was to proceed down the road to occupy a small town in the Vosges Mountains. The fifteen tanks of "C" company drove down the road in very dense fog on a cold morning. Suddenly we were fired on with 88mm cannon fire and mortars from the forests adjacent to the left of the road. All tanks except mine immediately turned their turrets to the left to return fire to the enemy hidden by the fog. My tank commander ordered me to turn my gun to the right. I protested but he said, "The Germans are tricky. They fire on you from one side and then attack you from the other." The company commander radioed, "What the hell are you doing?" None of our tanks were hit, thanks to the dense fog. I felt the first fear induced adrenalin rush.

My tank commander started to disassemble the 50 caliber machine gun after we reached the town. He spotted a girl, jumped out of the tank, and chased her down the road. The disassembled machine gun parts were left on the back deck of the tank. Within minutes we received orders to redeploy. A strong counter attack was coming. My tank commander was nowhere in sight. I was immediately promoted to tank commander. I reassembled the machine gun as we moved out without him. We never heard what happened to him thereafter. Eventually I realized how fortunate it was to have his poor judgment disclosed without loss of life. I felt the weight of the responsibilities so suddenly thrust upon me.

Following this engagement, our Company commander called us together to discuss what we had learned and what we could have done better. During this critique one of the loaders (who loads shell into the 75mm cannon) advised that there should be urinals in tanks. The spent shells are very hot when ejected after each shot and could cause some severe pain.

We fought our way through the Vosges Mountains into the rolling hills of the Alsace plain. I had been promoted to platoon sergeant by that time which carried a staff sergeant rating. A tank platoon consisted of five tanks under the command of a lieutenant. The platoon sergeant led a section of two of these tanks, the lieu-tenant the other three when the platoon needed to be separated.

Two Impulsive Acts

The German counter attack, the "Battle of the Bulge," had taken place and we were ordered to take up positions and to attack elsewhere. On January 12 we were ordered back to the Rittershoffen area because the Germans had broken through our defense lines near there. The five tanks of our platoon rounded a hill in echelon formation. My tank was positioned to the left and behind the lead tank. We spotted tanks and other vehicles moving too far away to be identified. "Are these ours or are they Germans?" I radioed back. "They appear to be ours." was the response.

We continued on course when our lead tank was hit by an anti tank shell and smoke began to pour out of its turret. Several of the crew managed to climb out of the turret and lay on its back deck, obviously hurt. Machine gun fire began to pour down on them. Without thinking I leapt out of my tank and crawled over to them, pulled them to the ground, used belts and whatever I could reach in my panic to put tourniquets on severed limbs and pulled them back onto my tank, bullets flying all around us. We quickly retreated behind the shelter of a mound. Medics were called and for the first time I became ill at the sight of the terrible injuries my friends suffered. As I slowly began to pull myself together I felt I was sitting on something very cold. A bullet had torn the seat of my pants. I was later advised that I was awarded a Bronze Star for heroism and that the Kansas City Star newspaper had published the following:

Our section of two tanks was assigned to support a battalion of the 342nd Infantry Regiment of the 86th Infantry Division at the end of March 1945.

This Infantry Division had just arrived from the United States and had not seen any combat. We moved constantly for two days without encountering any significant resistance. We suddenly came under fire as we moved forward toward Ingolstadt which was held by the Germans. The entire battalion scattered for shelter losing command control. No one knew the source of the enemy fire or if a possible German attack was eminent. Not only was our advance halted but also there was danger of having no organized line of defense should a Germans counter attack occur.

I left my tank and crawled up to a knoll to see if I could spot the source of the German fire and if there were any visible signs of a German attack. Flashes from four artillery pieces and several machine guns at the edge of a wooded area disclosed the sources. A search for the officer in charge of the infantry led me to a major seeking shelter under a viaduct. "I have found the source of the enemy fire. I will pull up my tanks and fire on them in 15 minutes to draw fire while you round up your units to move forward. I will cover you." The plan worked and Ingolstadt was captured. The Commanding General of the 86th Infantry Division learned of my action in support of his division's advance. He offered me a battlefield field commission to lieutenant in his infantry division. This recognition helped restore my self confidence but I declined the offer. I was trained in and had experience in tank warfare but lacked infantry training.

The Kansas City Star newspaper subsequently published my receiving a second Bronze Star.

These were not meditated heroic acts but were the impulsive and adrenaline charged actions of a 20 year old under stress. I became aware of the citations in the KC Star after I returned home. My parents had them mounted in a frame. 130

A Quick Decision

Our division was assigned to George Patton's Third army at the outbreak of the Battle of the Bulge. Our battalion was ordered to retreat from our defensive positions one icy cold and snowy night. One of our tank platoons was ordered to remain behind to provide rear guard action. They were ordered to retreat across the fields when they could no longer hear the sound of our retreating tanks. They had specific orders not to retreat down the road taken by the rest of us. They were to come across the field. Four to five inches of snow covered the ground with blowing snow beginning to form increasingly deeper snow drifts in some areas.

Captain Winiarczyk ordered me to post my tank at the point from which the rest of the retreating tank battalion would leave the road. They would cross the fields to form at a new defense line somewhere ahead. I was to stay to await the return of our tank platoon which was providing rear guard protection. "They have strict instructions not to come down the road and to maintain radio silence. We don't want the Germans to know we are pulling back. If you hear tanks coming down the road it will be the Germans. Get out of there in a hurry." were his orders. He pointed in the general direction our retreating battalion would be taking and asked that I guide the rear guard platoon in that direction were we able to get away. Radio silence was to be maintained. Soon the sounds and tracks of the retreating battalion's tanks disappeared in the blowing snow. We were alone. The short-lived silence was eerie.

I posted my tank in a position which would allow us to get away quickly. Armed with my submachine gun, I crawled into a snow covered ditch to wait for whatever might happen. It was pitch dark and visibility was only about 20 - 30 yards. How could we get away if the Germans could not be spotted through the blizzard in time? I repositioned my tank so that it would be hidden; hoping that an initial German advance would bypass us. I began to hear machine gun fire at some distance behind us. My first instinct was that we were being surrounded. My gunner, George Molnar, left the tank and crawled up next to me. "I'm not going to leave you out here alone." He said. This act touched me very deeply then as it still does today. I asked him to return to the tank. He would have to take command if anything happened to me.

It seemed like an eternity laying out there in the dark, snow driven, and cold night. Suddenly I could hear the sound of approaching tanks. These were coming down the road, not across the field. I had only seconds to flee or to risk stepping out on the road.

If they indeed were the Germans I was a dead man. If they were ours, their adrenaline laden flight could cause them to shoot anyone suddenly appearing on the road. If I fled they would certainly be lost and not survive the coming day. I silently said, "God be with me" and stepped into the road with a flashlight to signal the tanks to stop.

My tension suddenly eased as our tanks appeared through the snow whipped up by the ever increasing winds. I asked the lieutenant to follow my tank. I would lead them back across the fields to join the rest of our company. We started to lead in the direction to which Winiarczyk had generally pointed. I had no idea how many miles we would need to go, how narrow the areas in the defense line our company would be occupying, or where the Germans were. If we miss reuniting with our company on the line, would the other defenders assume that this is the anticipated German attack and open fire? Visibility was near zero.

The blowing snow had erased all traces of the path taken by our company. Increasingly deep snow drifts and ditches I could not see from the turret of my tank began to threaten our retreat. It would be a disaster to get our tanks stuck. I dismounted and began to walk ahead of the tanks to avoid snow covered gulleys and to find higher ground.

The resulting path was slow and torturous as we snaked our way through the blowing snow. Before long, George Molnar came from our tank me to tell me the lieutenant had radioed the captain to tell him that the idiot leading them had no idea where he was going and was going to get them all killed. "Tell the lieutenant that I will get them back," I asked George. George made several trips to report the lieutenant's continuous panic calls. "He told the captain that he will take his platoon and race past my tank." George told me on one of the last trips from our tank. It was shortly thereafter that the captain radioed the lieutenant, "Keep calm and keep following him. I can hear you approaching. And stay off the radio." That entire episode took no more than two hours, yet it seemed like a lifetime to me. Exhaustion hit me as we joined our defense line. A recommendation to receive the Silver Star for this action was submitted. It was declined at higher headquarters as no medals are granted for retreats.

A Loveable Rascal

Joe was the bow gunner on our tank in WW II. He loved to drink, was a clown and a character, and on the surface, immune to the fear which we all felt at times.

We had just captured a town in Alsace. It was common to have a lull of about 10 - 15 minutes before the Germans loosened a barrage of artillery fire into the defense position from which they were driven. During this lull Joe, who claimed to be a great cook, would forage for food, searching house by house. On occasion he would succeed, bringing some relief from the pervasive C rations, which were considerably less than a gourmet meal. Villagers in the Vosges Mountains preserved hard boiled eggs in brine and Joe had a nose for them.

True to form, Joe immediately left the tank and began his search for food. The German barrage started sooner than expected but that did not deter Joe from his quest. We saw him zigzag down the street chasing a chicken as shells began to burst around him.

He survived the shelling and that night said he was ready to treat us to a delicious meal. We expected chicken. One bite was enough. It was tough and had a very unsavory taste. He had caught a cat!

He was a dandy and a tippler but such a loveable rascal.

A Close Encounter

German Tiger tanks had been reported in the area. The Tiger tanks were superior to our Sherman tanks. Their 88 mm cannons easily pierced the thickest armor on our Sherman tanks from a greater distance than our 75mm cannons could reach.

I pulled my two tanks up a slope to where only our turrets were exposed. We spotted a Tiger tank crossing just 600 yards ahead of us, a clean shot! We fired two armor piercing shells at the side of the tank. Both tracer shells ricochet off the side of the tank. The Tiger turned his turret toward us to return fire with his 88 mm cannon. I ordered our tanks to withdraw below the ridge. My driver, Al Happel, quickly reversed our tank. The driver of the tank next to us was not as quick. A shot by the Tiger tank's 88 decapitated the tank commander. The resulting loss and shock to us all and particularly to the crew of the other tank, did not wear off very quickly. Imagine seeing the headless bleeding body of a comrade drop next to you. It soon stiffened our resolve to hit back as hard as possible.

I learned that we had to get much closer to a Tiger tank or to attack it from the rear where its armor was not as thick to knock it out. Bombing was the most effective means of knocking them out but we had to have air superiority and available aircraft in the area to do so.

The Futility of War

Abraham Hirsekorn, my great grandfather, served in the German Army in wars against Denmark in 1864, against Austria in 1866, and against France in 1870/71.

Julius Hirsekorn, Abraham's son and my grandfather, served in the
German Army under three Kaisers, Wilhelm I (1871 - 1888),
Friedrich III (1888) and Wilhelm II (1888-1918)

Fred Hirsekorn served in the US Army in WWII fighting the Germans. 1943-1946

My father, Ludwig Hirsekorn, Julius's son, served in a Field Artillery
Regiment in the German army during World War I and saw service in France,
Belgium, and Russia. He was awarded an Iron Cross for his service.

At least three generations had fought for Germany, the fourth generation fought against Germany. This makes wars seem so absurd and so senseless.

It certainly raises the question of why do wars occur, each war causing death and destruction. Wars have ravaged human beings throughout history causing death and injuries not only to combatants but also to millions of men, women, and children; civilians not directly involved in the conflict. If both sides of a conflict knew in advance just how devastating a war would be, why couldn't they accept negotiating the postwar outcome without having to actually pay the horrible cost of fighting a war? It is because each side will always claim that morality justifies their fight. The aggressor will have an overly optimistic assessment of the outcome of hostilities.

Currently there are 8 major wars, defined as inflicting 1,000 battlefield deaths per year, with 27 other conflicts in progress. The goal of offensive wars is submission, assimilation or destruction of another group. The goal of defensive wars is simply the repulsion of the offensive force or survival itself.

One need only identify the universal reasons for wars to arrive at a very pessimistic and unhappy conclusion. Power hungry leaders who have no regard for life are one of the main driving forces. They grasp on poor economic conditions, with promises of a better life for their population, to rise to power. History has shown that no wars can begin without the support of the general populace.

Once in power they impose their will on those who put them in power through intimidation. Napoleon and Hitler are good examples of such leaders who sought conquest and thus war.

Religion is another main driving force. These differences are more difficult to 'negotiate' to settle outcomes without bloodshed. A religious war is a war caused by, or justified by, religious differences. It can involve one state with an established religion against another state with a different religion or a different sect within the same religion, or a religiously motivated group attempting to spread its faith by violence, or to suppress another group because of its religious beliefs or practices. The Muslim conquests, the French Wars of Religion, the Crusades, and the Reconquista are frequently cited historical examples.

Power hungry leaders with psychologically abnormal disregard for human life have and will always emerge. Was Saddam Hussein of Iraq and are Ahmadinejad of Iran and Kim Jong-Il of North Korea currently such leaders? Religious differences will always exist.

There will always be those who value life and freedom and are willing to make the sacrifice to defend it.

Thank God for the USA.

Unsung Heroes

This morning's e-mails contained tributes to the servicemen and women who have and who are sacrificing so much to keep us safe and to free those who are oppressed. These are well deserved tributes. There are however many unsung heroes whose sacrifices are not equally recognized.

A close friendship developed with my roommate Don Reaugh from Newton, Kansas, while in ASTP (Army Specialized Training Program) at Ohio State University in 1945. Don and I were transferred to the 14th Armored Division when this Army program was abruptly discontinued. Don was assigned to the 19th armored infantry battalion and I to the 25th tank battalion. Within weeks we were in combat in Europe.

One of the bitterest battles occurred during the Bulge in January 1945. It was not until I happened to meet some of the fellows from Don's battalion several weeks there after that I learned that Don had been killed not more than about 10 yards from my tank. We could not see the infantry in fox holes in a ditch ahead of us. We were buttoned up (hatches closed) due to the heavy machine gun fire and airbursts of artillery fire we were receiving. Machine gun fire had caught Don across the knees. Unable to crawl out along with the others he bled to death.

I was deeply stricken. Returning home after the war, I was obsessed with the thought that I should do something. During the summer of 1946 the thought occurred to me to meet Don's father, to pay tribute to Don, and the exceptional friend he became and person he was.

I drove to the 200 miles to Newton, Kansas. What can I possibly say to him? It became increasingly more difficult to find the words as I approached Newton.

Shall I show him the pictures I brought of Don? Should he ask me how he was killed, I would tell him that it was quick.

I was directed to a small grocery store which his father owned.

After he finished waiting on one of his customers I introduced myself.

"Mr. Reaugh, I came to pay my respects. Don was a close friend with whom I served in the 14th Armored Division."

It was as though I had hit him with a baseball bat. After a moment he shouted,

"Why weren't you killed instead of him?"

I was stunned. I muttered, "I'm sorry" and left for the long hot drive back to Kansas City.

A whirlwind of thoughts accompanied my drive home. It was not until later that I realized that there are many, like Mr. Reaugh, who was deeply wounded by the war. Their wounds are not visible until the scar tissue is torn from wounds which linger for years.

These are also heroes to whom tribute should be paid and whose sacrifices should be equally recognized over the years.

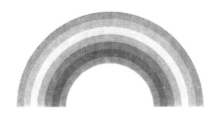

CREATIVE WRITING

On being Creative

We are all creative. Of course the nature of our creativity may not only impact our family and friends but also on the wider community. It also depends on the age at which we demonstrate our creativity.

Take our three year old great grandson, for example. Lying on his back on the carpeted living room floor, he looks directly at you, raises his shoeless foot and slowly pushes against the tall and narrow stand holding a flower pot, tipping it over, scattering the flowers and dirt all across the carpet. Now, I am not entirely without some inventiveness, but I could never create such an endeavor. Were I to do so, I am sure that the outcome would be entirely different.

A hypothetical example. Valentine's Day, my wife's birthday, or an anniversary rolls around, and suddenly I lose all creativeness. Well, not entirely. I call on one or more of my daughters to see if, during one of their shopping trips together, they have heard my wife mention some things she might like to have. She often lets our daughters know when she sees something she likes. Were this writing to be true, having my wife read this could also create an undesirable outcome, quite different than if were to lay on the floor and tip the flower pot over. (Ain't creating fiction fun? One can be bold and fearless.)

That leads me to the point. Modern medicine has, over the past few years, recognized the therapeutic value of creative writing. Creative writing has been added to the treasure chest of medical services provided for patients. Doctors have recognized that writing can contribute to healing. Pen and paper are trusted friends which keep confidential one's deepest thoughts, worries, and emotional pains. Some real, some imagined. Once down in writing, the problems seem to be put into proper perspective.

The creative writing thought process becomes like tapping into a cold keg of beer. It releases pressure which has built up, refreshes as it is consummated, and it produces an aura of self discovery and relief.

The difference is that drinking deeply of creative writing is empowering without causing unbalancing intoxication.

The Early Writing Obstacle

The first time I danced it was like a drunk stumbling down a muddy cobble stone street. Taking a dancing class seemed to be the answer. With time, I not only danced better but also began to really enjoy it. Still my early reputation preceded me. "May I have this dance?" I politely asked a good dancer at one of the high school dances. "Sorry, I have a headache" she replied. Two minutes later she was dancing with someone else. Never heard that an analgesic could work so fast.

Attempting to write my first essay in high school, my pen stumbled on every word, stuck on every sentence as though glued to the page as I struggled to articulate the issue. It was like my early dancing experience. I should have asked the girl which analgesic she took!

I did meet a girl who was a delightful dance partner and who eventually became my life's partner as well.

Since dancing class helped my dancing, a high school English composition class should help my writing, I thought. I chose it as an elective. The teacher focused on proper sentence structure, accurate punctuation, syntax, etc. Somehow this didn't exactly 'lubricate my pen' to dance across the page!

My education and my industrial experience made writing mandatory but often a real drudgery. I was not even aware that writing could be fun.

It was not until I was 86 years old that I discovered the 'analgesic' which gave flight to my pen, a creative writing class attended by seven octogenarians, taught by Minnesota Loft Instructor, Peter Blau. It loosened the shackles to let my imagination take flight.

The joy and grace of dancing with my wife however now only remains deeply etched in my memory.

Landing Words on Paper

A blank sheet of paper lies on my desk arrogantly staring me in the face. It was as though it dared me to smudge its pristine face with words. I rise to the challenge.

My pen lands a few words on the page and my mind immediately feels like a plane landing on a freshly poured concrete runway, the wheels sinking in slush.

This is going to be combat! I'll not surrender to a blank sheet of paper! I'll call in two helicopters to lift me out of the concrete, wait until it sets, circle the enemy, and then land on it with a vengeance.

What words can I etch on the surface of this defiant sheet, angry words, loving words? Neither fit the occasion.

My mind slowly clears as I circle above the prey. Diplomacy, not fighting this challenge will lead to a solution. Think of the paper, along with your pen, as friends who try to free the shackles of your mind. You might be delighted with what lurks inside.

Just in case though, have your paper shredder handy.

Why Do I Write?

I write because it provides an escape
Into a world which is ever pleasant to take.
Away from the chaos and daily strife,
Where imagination and fun come truly alive.

There are no ceilings to contain my flight;
No one to say, "No that isn't right."
I do not write for the public domain
Or for fame and richness to eventually gain.

With paper and pen poised and ready to soar,
A jarring pause; where do I start on this chore?
Where is that spark which is sure to ignite
That creative fire by which I shall write?

Is it something I've read or heard someone say
Which can start my pen on its meandering way?
Is the spark an experience which I have had?
Or a children's story with a moral clad.

Perhaps it's a prompt which we are presented
Which leads to a poem which can be invented.
Seattle won the Superbowl, now that is new
It is a poem I would much like to pursue.

My pen starts to quiver but will not start,
As though to say, "I thought you're smart.
Your memory must be completely depleted,
That is a poem you've just completed."

A Wonderful Escape

Torn quadriceps from a fall and bound to an electric scooter on the second floor of our home I soon got cabin fever. How I wished to escape to some of my favorite places. I loved the quiet and beauty of the Colorado Rocky Mountain lakes, mirroring the surrounding snow capped peaks on their blue calm surfaces, and the rustle of the leaves awakened by the gentle breezes. But travel is out, only the memories continue. Perhaps writing about these memories would, at least temporarily, relieve my sense of imprisonment.

Sitting here in front of the computer, the keyboard is staring up at me challenging me to get started. I lean back waiting for the ideas to flow. I look down and there is that keyboard sneering at me as though saying, "Hah, I got you this time."

I said "Well, Mr. keyboard, that isn't going to happen. You are not going to win."

My daughter walks in. "I thought I heard you were talking to someone. Are you talking to the computer?" she asked.

"No, I am talking to the keyboard."

She looked astonished and shook her head. As she left I heard her say, "Mom, you had better get dad some help. He's talking to his keyboard."

Football, that's it! I can really enjoy and get lost watching football. A quick check of the TV sports schedule…nothing, not even any replay of games. Music; listening to music, from Strauss waltzes to the Rag time rhythm of Scott Joplin is always a pleasant escape. Wouldn't you know it; I couldn't find any of our recordings.

Frustrated I looked down at the computer keyboard. I was surprised to find that the keyboard's attitude had changed. Perhaps it sensed that competition was brewing for it now greeted me with a smile as though to say, "Try me. Perhaps I can offer you a diversion." "What changed your mind," I asked the keyboard. "Never mind let's just travel together." Indeed, together we began to write. It provided a wonderful escape.

I was careful however not to speak to the keyboard too loud. My daughter might be listening.

The Rhythm

I'd like to write a poem,
The rhythm beats in my heart;
But I don't know how to get goin'
So I turn to these prompts for a start.

This morn *when I looked in the mirror*
For the poem which may lurk therein,
Looking back, very much to my chagrin,
Was an ogre I wouldn't even want as my kin.

It took courage to write
After seeing that vision.
So I quickly took flight
To avoid substantial derision.

But the rhythm won't stop, it continues to throb.
My search continues among the various prompts.
It cannot be such an overwhelming job
The urge will find a way thru the swamps.

Pastures of plenty should be a good source
To give vent to the rhythm within,
So I proceeded without any remorse
To search for a poem therein.

In *A place of imagination* I would surely find
Where a rainbow touches the grounds;
Where wishes at least bring some peace of mind
Where harmony among all people abounds.

I hope for this dream to come true and soon
So future generations will not live in fear
After all we've already sent a man to the moon
Why can't we achieve this objective more dear?

Thank you to those in our world who try
To bring freedom and peace on this earth
And may the rhythm in my heart beat also apply
To bring harmony to my little world find worth.

A written Pilgrimage

A pilgrimage is usually understood to be
A journey to a place most wondrous to see.
One feels the surrounding quite arousing
The spiritual lift to be equally quenching.

I found a closer pilgrimage we can make,
Into one's own mind and there to awake
That wonderful feeling that time will submerge
And a calming image will slowly emerge.

I took such a pilgrimage one sunny day
And vowed to record every step of the way.
With pencil and paper ready at hand
I wandered toward this mystical land.

I closed my eyes to shut out distraction
And then to record the astounding action.
I opened the door to my mind's wondrous chamber
And started my pilgrimage with pencil and paper.

With each step I took much to my chagrin,
I heard only an echo, agin and agin,
Resound in the empty space between my ears,
That was not a good destination it so appears.

What can I write about this hopeful expedition
When the journey has been such a dismal mission?
So I bring to these pages all I've written
About this pilgrimage. Oh boy, I am stricken.

Don Quixote

The assignment to write on, *"Describe the perfect Day"*,
And, *"What I what want my words to say,"*
Goad me to become quite elegantly poetic
And try to create a long lasting epic.

Like Don Quixote I mount my steed,
To my lack of talent I give no heed.
I charge the windmill with mindless speed
To write an epic about these prompts, indeed.

Just what do I want my words to say
When my day had started in such a bad way?
I had looked out the window at two feet of snow
With the outside temperature at forty below.

So I went back to bed and lo and behold,
A whole new vista began to unfold.
I dreamt I had won the lottery big,
Now there is something I really can dig!

Then a hand shook me gently and softly said,
"Your class in the den is reading ahead."
I rushed into the room, pajamas and all
To shock the class with words to enthrall.

I had charged the windmill with a result quite akin,
To feeling like crawling deep into my skin.
Then a voice awoke me, "Dinner is ready, come while it's hot.
You have a writing class next week." as though I forgot.

Now I've expounded on both prompts for next week,
And have fallen off my donkey and am left quite weak,
My creativity is exhausted but now that it's done,
It's been a wild ride, but it sure has been fun!

An Adapted Poem

Tennyson's poem	The writer's adaptation
Charge of the Light Brigade	*Charge of the kid's Brigade*
published December 9, 1854	never published

'Forward, the Light Brigade!'	Forward, the eager children surged
Was there a man dismayed?	With not a single one dismayed.
Not tho' the soldiers knew	Onward, onward, all were urged,
Some one had blundered:	by candy so freely displayed.
Theirs not to make reply	Can it be eaten without having to pay?
Theirs not to reason why,	There was no the reason, it is the way.
Theirs but to do and die:	It's there o take, and so they stuffed
Into the valley of Death	Into their little tummies
Rode the six hundred.	That delicious stuff.
Cannon to the right of them,	Candy to the right of them
Cannon to the left of them,	Candy to the left of them
Cannon in front of them	Candy in front of them
Volleyed and thundered;	they continue to plunder

Stormed at with shot and shell,

Boldly they rode and well,

Into the jaws of Death,

Rode the six hundred.

Though the proprietor began to yell;

Boldly they ate, and well;

but their stomachs soon did rebel.

In Search for an Oasis

I often feel as though my words are like nomads wandering in the desert, with no coherent destiny, on an endless search for an oasis. I long for each word to be like a note in a musical composition which, in chorus with other words, creates the pleasant aura which transports one from the everyday turmoil to a calm haven, to have each destiny enrich the moment, to bring a smile to replace a frown, and to make it a pleasure to read.

Each word in my sonata must clearly and tersely sound its clarion voice to contribute the exact and harmonious connotation intended. As I read the first draft of my writings it often sounds more like a cacophony in a chicken coop rather than the symphony I intended to write.

How did the great composers, Bach, Beethoven, Strauss, and others approach their creations? Did they have a destiny in mind? Did they have a mood they wanted to create before they started putting down the notes? Did they have a message they wanted to convey?

How about the great writers, Poe, Faulkner, Fitzgerald, Hemmingway, and others? How did they start a composition? Did they have a message in mind? How frustrated were they as they searched for the destination? Incidentally, these among the top 15 20th Century American writers were all alcoholics. Should I start drinking? Not aspiring to such excellence in writing perhaps this approach is not recommended.

Slowly, as I begin to gather the eggs in the chicken coop, I begin to realize that my mind and my imagination can lead me toward an oasis. I may not always get quite there but I get some comfort that my pencil can roam to eventually shorten the distance.

Her Trembling Lips

Her trembling lips and melancholy eyes struck me when I first saw her. I became immediately enamored. Well, I would not say trembling lips but rather wet lips. She was beautiful and emotional.

We established a long relationship. I loved the way she responded to me. She eagerly awaited my return home from work each day. She would jump all over me, her joy to see me touching me deeply. I would pet her and the delight we each felt was evident.

She loved to play.

I would throw a ball across the room and she would chase it, bring it back to me, tail wagging, barking for another throw.

Ruby Red Lips

She had ruby red lips although I must say,
They totally eclipsed her in every way.

She believed in the tactic that if you felt low,
Put on some lipstick and the feeling will go.

But each kiss on the cheek left a bright red mark,
Horizontal or oblique as though applied as a lark.

Friends were branded with every peck
Which haphazardly landed from cheek to neck.
From layers of lipstick she had heavily applied,
The transfer was quick and recipients just sighed.

Not resigned to this fate a club they did form,
Open to all whose dignity was thus shorn.

From dues collected each holiday,
A light colored lipstick she was given a gift.
"To help smooth your way.
We hope it will give us all a lift."

Jump off and fly?

One sunny fall morning, I found myself walking along the ridge of the White Cliffs of Dover. A gentle breeze was blowing from the south and I could see south across the blue waters of the English Channel all the away to France. Looking straight down 350 feet I could barely make out a few people walking along the shore wading through the surf. I recalled that a glider had crossed the channel to France many years ago.

The wind picked up and inflated my windbreaker and almost lifted me. I began to wonder, am I ready to jump off the cliff and fly? Perhaps the wind will let me rise sufficiently high to be able to glide to the French shore. Could I make it all the way across the channel to France?

Of course I can. It has been done with a glider! I opened my windbreaker to get more surfaces to lift me and ran into the wind to get off the ground. I could not believe it. I was flying, soaring to great heights! What a wonderful floating feeling.

There was only one problem. The wind blew me north into the mainland instead of gliding south toward France. I was heading toward Heathrow airport. Luckily I had my cell phone to call the control tower at the airport to get clearance to land.

"This is Eagle 1 requesting clearance to land."

"We do not see you on our radar, Eagle 1. What are your coordinates?" came the tower's response.

"I don't know. This is an emergency and I see planes all around me and the landing strip ahead. I must land."

"We have visual sighting of a small dot in the sky. That must be you. Emergency equipment will await you on the ground." answered the tower. "Use runway 231 west." From up high I could see the blinking lights of the fire engines and the ambulances as they raced along the runway.

Suddenly the wind stopped and I plummeted downward thinking that the end is near. I closed my eyes. I felt the impact as I slammed into cold water of the Longford River near the airport.

Cold, I opened my eyes. I had fallen out of bed, the cool breeze from the ceiling fan continuing to chill me.

Thank goodness it was a dream. The English police could have arrested me for not filing a flight plan, for flying without a license and for disrupting the traffic at one of the world's busiest airports.

A Confusing Language

English is a very confusing language for foreigners to learn. Imagine that you are emigrating from another country and unable to speak the English.

You learn that the word wrinkle means a line or crease between the folds in the skin. Then you learn that you have a wrinkle in your plan to obtain citizenship. What? You cannot figure out what this means. I don't have any creases in my skin? What does that have to do with my citizenship application anyway?

Then you learn that a wrinkle can also mean a messy fold in cloth or paper. Aha! The application for citizenship has been crumpled. That should not be a problem.

Next you are told that a new wrinkle has been found which will delay proceeding with your application. Confusion abounds.

You come home from your night shift work before your wife leaves for her day time job at the marina. She was visibly upset. "The English Language is impossible to learn." she grumbled, shaking her head. "Someone at work had said that, there was a **row** amongst the **row** of oarsmen about how to **row**. Not only does the word **r o w** have different meanings but it isn't even pronounced the same way!"

The plural of tooth is pronounced teeth; then why isn't the plural of booth beeth; one moose, 2 meese?"

She is frustrated as she puts on her boots. "English is a crazy language to boot."

There are no eggs in eggplant, no apple or pine in pineapple, no ham in hamburger.

Writers write but fingers don't fing and grocers don't groce. If a vegetarian eats vegetables, what does a humanitarian eat? Are a wise man and a wise guy the same?

The wrinkle is that English was invented by people which reflect the creativity of the human race…which is not a race after all.

The Use of Words

Since the birth of the first of our four daughter in 1951 I have witnessed (and experienced) the rise of women's liberation. History has shown that whenever a pendulum swings too far for any injustice, it always swings back too far before it reaches equilibrium. Has this been the case for women's liberation?

Let us look deeper. How many words end in 'her' and how many in "him"? Extensive research shows that 376 words end with 'her' while only 16 end with 'him. No one ever alerted the general public of this discretely hidden inequity in favor of women.

This led me to wonder who originated words. Was it women? How could it be?

Back during the Neanderthal period a male would simply drag a woman of his choice by the hair and drag her into his cave. No thoughts of women's liberation then. And no words were needed. (Men are becoming bald to prevent women retaliating the same way.) Back then, cave men drew pictures on the wall of caves to express and record their experiences. No words. (Another pendulum. Today we strive to paint pictures with words.)

In the English language alone, 1,022,000 words been invented by 2012 and about 15 new ones are being added every day! And some are so long. Who invented and keeps inventing all these words? And so many good words are being misused. For example, in Richard Sheridan's 1775 play *The Rivals*, Mrs. Malaprop, the leading character, had a propensity to use so many already existing words, it made one wonder what it is she wants to say. For example: "*Try to forget *this fellow...... <u>illiterate</u> him from your memory"* or, *"Why, murder is the matter! Slaughter is the matter! But he can tell you the perpendiculars."*

Even today famous people use the wrong words resulting in malapropisms. For example: *George Bush: "It will take time to restore chaos and order,"* or by others

"If Mauer had tried to catch that ball it would have decapitated his hand."

It gets harder and more complicated to understand and to hang on to the pendulums in my life. Let's at least not invent any more words! I've already developed a case of Hippopotomonstrosesquipedaliophobia....fear of long words.

Lost and Obsolete Words

Jim drove from the **lubitorium** to take his little son Eric to the **tragematopolist,** even though he felt a little **wabbit** with a **woofit** coming on. Brutus, the owner, was quite **perissologic** and a **pronk.** Jim, a **polihistor** was **gradgring.** He did not relish going on this errand, but he had promised little Eric he would do so.

Brutus was **bucculent** when he saw Jim enter. The last time Jim was there Brutus's **acrasia** had upset Jim so much, that a return visit was certainly not expected. Jim was **yslogistic** at the time and Brutus became **pococurantish** and his service was **testudineous.** That had annoyed Jim even more. Brutus thought that visit had brought their relationship to a **quatervois.**

Not wanting to rupture their relationship further, Brutus decided on **ascasis.** He knew that Jim had **emacity** and it would be **badot** to irritate Jim further.

Translation:

*Jim drove from the **filling station** to take his little son Eric to the **candy store,** even though he felt a little **under the weather** with a **headache** coming on. Brutus the owner was a **foolish person** quite **long winded.** Jim was interested only in **cold hard facts** and a **well educated person.** Jim did not relish going on this errand but he had promised little Eric he would do so.*

*Brutus was **wide mouthed** when he saw Jim enter. The last time Jim was there Brutus's **loss of self control** had upset Jim so much that a return visit was certainly not expected. Jim was **disapproving** at the time and Brutus became **indifferent** and is service was **slow as a tortoise.** That* *annoyed Jim even more. Brutus thought that visit had brought their relationship to a* **crossroad.**

Not wanting to rupture their relationship further Brutus decided on **practicing self control***. He knew that Jim had* **a fondness for buying things** *and it would be* **foolish** *to irritate Jim further.*

The visit might have gone well but this writer has become tongue tied trying to pronounce all of these lost and obsolete words and finds pleasure that they no longer exist.

Obsolete but not Forgotten

English was first spoken in England by Germanic tribes in the fifth century AD. It was known as Old English. Since that time, it has grown from 50,000 or so words to over 1 million today. It continues to grow each year and has almost doubled in the last 50 years. Examples of the hundreds new words added to the Oxford dictionaries last year included, **byod** (bring you own drink), **fil** (father in law) also **mil**, **bil**, **sil**, **ldr** (long distant relationship), **srsly** (seriously), **tl:dr** (too long didn't read) and **balayage** (a technique for highlighting hair to create a graduated, natural looking effect.) Texting and cosmetic practices are invading the dictionary.

The average educated adult is said to have access to about 2000 words, if which 200 are used. Who needs more? But they keep on coming. There is even a movement afoot to add obsolete and deleted words back to the dictionary. Here is what that would sound like:

Dining with friends the night before had left me feeling **crapulous**. **Curmuring** soon came to my attention. I had been **gorgonized** by a **snoutfair, groaking, jurbling** as I poured wine into my glass.

I hurriedly got dressed and stepped out into the **snowbroth**. The **apricity** was refreshing. The **circumjacence** in the office soon quenched this feeling.

My **cockarowse** had been **hugger-mungaring** which **jargogled** me. The **twattle** in the office was that he was silently eyeing my **callipygian**. Finally the **slubberdegullion**, a **beef-witted,**

and jullox cockalorum, with elflock , who was really only a **quokermsodger** controlled by his boss told me I was fired. He said his boss had read an article by a **spermologer** which accused me of **peculation**.

It came as a **curglaff**. My denying the accusation soon descended into **brabbling**.

Sadly I packed my belongings and again stepped out into the sunlit **snowbroth.** Much to my surprise the **cokarowse's** boss awaited me. He made me an offer I could not turn down.

What does it mean? Translation:

Dining with my friends the night before had left me *feeling ill from eating and drinking too much. A low rumbling sound produced by the bowel* soon came to my attention. While eating I had been *mesmerized* by a *good looking person* and was *silently watching him hoping to be invited to join him at his table, my hand unsteady* while I poured wine into my glass.

I hurriedly got dressed and stepped out into the morning's *fresh melted snow. The sun's warmth on a cold winter day* was refreshing. The *atmosphere* in the office soon quenched this feeling.

My *boss* had *been secretively watching me* which *confused* me. The *gossip* in the office was that he was silently eyeing my *beautifully shaped buttocks. Finally the slovenly, stupid, and fat guy with tangled hair,* who was *only a puppet on the strings controlled by his boss*, told me that I was fired. He said that his boss read an article by a *gossip columnist* who accused me of *shop lifting*. It came as a *shock*. My denying the accusations soon descended into *arguing about inconsequentials*.

Sadly, I packed my belongings and again stepped into the *sunlit melted snow*. Much to my surprise, my *boss's boss* awaited me. He made me an offer I could not turn down.

Paraprosdokians

I love to write. Sometimes it is hard to get started. An unexpected event occasionally breaks through this roadblock, like last night's evening news. The anchorman began with 'Good Evening' and then proceeded to tell us why it isn't. It was a real paraprosdokian, a situation or sentence in which the latter part is surprising or unexpected.

I recalled that Winston Churchill loved paraprosdokians. I searched and found a number of them. Some examples:

Where there is a will......I want to be in it.

Relating to the news lately; "Behind every successful man is a woman. Behind the fall of a successful man is usually another woman."

You don't need a parachute to skydive. You only need a parachute to skydive twice.

A bus station is where the bus stops and the train station is where the train stops. On my desk I have a work station.

When the engine on your air plane fails you always have enough power left .....to get to the scene of the crash.

The crash truck arrives, the first responder sees the bloodied pilot and asks," What happened?" The pilot responds: "Beats the hell outta me. ...I just got here myself."

I love paraprosdokians. Thank goodness for the evening news. It made my whimsical pen come alive.

Savor the Moments

A warm breeze awoke the tree from its winter's rest.
It stretched its limbs to shake off the cold,
And avidly yearned for a cardinal to nest
After its life's blood helps its leaves to unfold.

I sit at my window to await that sight
When the sun shine embraces the tree,
Now fully adorned, and a cardinal in flight
Looks for where her next nest should be.

The weeks go by under my diligent watch,
As the masked cardinal tends to her eggs,
Under the protective leaves of that wonderful tree
Where the young hatch test their wobbly legs.

I savored each moment from the awakening of the tree
To the budding of its leaves after its winter's nap;
Through the flight of the newborns from the tree's cozy nest
To explore the world and its wonders to tap.

The Musical Tree

The sounds of birds cheerfully chirping away in a tree outside my window awoke me, as the sun rose this morning. How wonderful to lay there and enjoy natures symphony. The leaves of the tree danced in the breeze to the rhythm of the birds' melody. It was as though the entire tree was enjoying their musical performance. Who orchestrates the Oriole, Robin, and Finch musicians and decides on their repertoire?

I look forward to this gift every spring when the birds return to build their nests in the same beautiful, oval-shaped, tree with its bright green leaves in full splendor. Do the birds return to this beautiful tree each year because they enjoy it as much as I do? Or does the tree maintain its beautiful shape in order to attract the same bird musicians each year?

Do the birds view the tree as part of their home or is it only the safe nesting which attracts them? How far did they migrate during the winter and how did they find their way back to the same tree in the spring? Surely these are the same birds which return each year. The orchestration can only come from practiced musicians who have played together for some time.

This special treat is enjoyed for too short a time during the year. The musicians depart for distant lands as freezing temperatures, sleet, and snow descend on the tree. When the sun rises each winter day I see the sparkling ice encrusted arms reach for the sky as though the tree is establishing a beacon to guide the birds to it for the following spring.

The Sound of Silence

What is silence?
Is it the absence of sound?
Is it a wall that separates?
Is it solitude and loneliness?
Is it moments which are awkward?
What is silence?

Silence is a feeling.
It touches the soul and warms the heart
And captures ones spirit as nothing else can.
It heightens the senses and makes us aware,
Of the beauty around us as nothing else can.
Silence is a feeling.

Silence is a haven.
From the cacophony of the day
To let us sense the beauty of nature,
And there feel the warmth which abounds
To illuminate our lives with perspective.
Silence is a haven.

Silence is an emotion.
You smile across the table
At your other who quietly reads.
That is quality time wrapped by silence

Which the warmth of your smile implies.
Silence is an emotion.

A lone walk through the forest lanes,
To a brook flowing calmly below,
As a rustling green canopy enfolds you,
The blue sky embracing all that you see,
And all of nature reaches out to grant you
The silence of a spiritual sensation.

When noise pollution overwhelms you,
Then to the world of silence do go;
For that is where serenity is embracing
It's a place where perspective is found
In a world where only nature abounds.
Silence is a refuge.

Pearls Upon a Page

Paper and pencil are ready to produce a gem as I place the first pearl of prose upon the page. As I ponder how to continue, lo and behold, the pearl rolls off the page much to my chagrin. What I thought was a lustrous idea ended up rolling across the floor, disappearing into the fog of my creativity.

With such a dismal start, how am I ever going to create and string a number pearls together into a beautiful necklace of prose? Even an oyster, when irritated, can produce only one pearl and that takes a long time.

Well, I am not an oyster. There are a few people who irritate me enough to quickly produce a dozen pearls at a time. I should be able to adorn the page with a string of these pearls! They are not the types of pearls my pen wants to string on the paper however.

My mind quickly wanders into another quagmire. There are so many different types of pearls, so many different sizes, shapes, with different lusters, colors and surface purity. To place these pearls on one page would require such small fonts that it could not be read.

My impatient pencil, sensing the passing of time, urges me to look in an entirely different direction to get us out of this quagmire. "What is the common component of all pearls?" it asks. Aha; It is that the all are made of minute forms of calcium carbonate. The page now chimes in with, "You chemists aren't very romantic, are you?" That's all I need, the paper chiming in with snide remarks. I knew that I was on the right track but sat there completely stymied. I am still sitting here with an empty page.

"There are pearls all of which have one thing in common," my pencil calmly suggested. "What kind of pearls are these?"

Somewhere out of the depth crept "Pearls of Wisdom." That broke the log jam thanks to the snide paper and the smart pencil. They all have worthwhile concepts.

For example, there is Benjamin Disraeli who once said: "The greatest good one can do for another is not just to share ones riches but to reveal to him his own."

"The writer who postpones the recording of his thoughts uses an iron which is too cool to burn a hole." said Henry David Thoreau.

Or, "The perfect summer day is when the sun is shining, the breeze is blowing, the birds are singing, and the lawn mower is broke," said Fred.

As I find more and more pearls of wisdom I place them on the page. What they have in common is that they form a string of beautiful and inspiring thoughts to be worn in my memory.

The Pencils Job

My pencils are usually in a good mood and will sometimes make the page really come alive. Today, however they were in a grumpy mood. The page just laid there in a coma. Exasperated, I gathered them up.

"Listen you guys; if you don't snap out of your slump, we won't be able to meet the publication deadline. We are tethered together and I have reached the limit of my patience. I may need to take some drastic measures which would make you undergo some very painful sharpening. But first tell me what is bothering you."

Slowly they grudgingly spoke up. One of the group said, "I've been in your desk for a long time and feel I am forgotten."

"Yah," said another, "I have been under your desk for a long time and think you don't care anymore."

"What I write isn't published," piped up another.

The shortest of the bunch mumbled, "I'm just about written out."

"Know this." I answered. "You will all be writing soon. Everything you do leaves a mark. If you are not happy with what you write, you can always try again. The imaginative pages you have written, even you Shorty, should give you confidence that more are lurking inside of you.

Remember, what makes you a pencil is not what's outside of you; it's what's inside of you. So get the lead out and try to be the very best pencil in the world. It's what you were put on this earth to be."

The Treasure Hunt

I collect pen and paper and sat on my patio on a warm sunny spring morning, poised to have the pen record a Pulitzer Prize for fiction. Time passes and the pen still in my hand has not moved. I could hear the happy muffled sound of children playing in the distance. The warm breeze rustled the leaves on the trees and two blue jays flying overhead stopped to sing their soft, quiet conglomeration of clicks, chucks, whirrs, whines, and liquid notes. Such a beautiful relaxing scene by which to let the pen create.

Suddenly the pen touches the paper and started to write, all on its own as if guided by magic. The blue jays stopped their songs and became fascinated by the movement of the pen. I was amazed by the story the pen was writing. It wrote that a map could be found behind an old framed picture on sale at a garage sale in the neighborhood. The map would show where two bank robbers buried their loot in an abandoned gravel pit several miles from here.

Leaving the pen and paper I looked in the newspaper and sure enough; there was an ad for a garage sale only two blocks away. I drove to the sale. There among other musty items was a framed picture of an old bank building no longer in existance. Could this be for real? Excited but not wanting to show how eager I was to purchase the picture I began to bargain with the owner. He eventually sold it to me for one dollar.

My heart was beating as I rushed home. Gently removing the faded and fragile picture backing I found a map. It too had deteriorated with age but the direction to the gravel pit, where the cash from a major robbery of the bank was buried, was still legible. I could feel my heart beating fast and loud.

Grabbing a shovel from our garage I quickly drove to the gravel pit. There as shown on the map was the spot the money was buried. Digging vigorously, I hit something hard. Dripping with perspiration, I dug up a suitcase. In it were hundreds of tens, fifty and one hundred dollar bills. I quickly loaded the money into the trunk of my car feeling dizzy with excitement. Suddenly I felt someone grab me from behind.

It was my wife. She said, "Honey I'm glad I came out to the patio when I did. You must have fallen asleep and were about to fall off your chair." As though laughing, there on the floor laid the untouched pen and paper.

The Wise Person Within

I have searched whether or not there is really a wise person within. I was told that writing can access that wisdom.

Pen and paper in hand I eagerly started the search. I waited and waited for my pen to access what there is within. Minutes elapsed and …nothing. Could it be that my pen cannot access what isn't there?

I persisted. After a while I found myself doodling squares, circles, and arrows. Strange. The arrows all pointed in the same direction. Following that line took me to a picture of my wife with our four daughters.

Writing, in this case the doodling, accessed the answer. There may not be a wise person within. However I take solace in the fact that I was at least smart enough to marry the right girl who, with our daughters, are some of the wisest persons in my life.

The pen was right.

Why Do I Care

There are many things in our world today which cause great concern. We are concerned about global warming, the adversarial nature of our Congress, the volatility of the stock market, Iran and the nuclear threat, major natural disasters, the energy crisis, hunger around the world, the economy, terrorism, globalization, unemployment, pollution, shortage of clean water which takes the lives of over 14,000 people every day, just to mention a few.

Before asking why we should care, perhaps it would be worth thinking about the fact that we do care. We are emotional and moral beings. We simply aren't capable of observing other people's behavior or threatening conditions without reacting emotionally and morally. We care because we want to help. When we cease to care altogether, we cease to function as humans.

The fact that we do care helps define us as being empathetic, giving, tender, reflective and nurturing. We care so much about this beautiful wonderful world. We have to be realistic however, that there is only so much which our caring can accomplish.

Why do I care about writing? At least I can try to paint a picture with words that convey an experience or a feeling. I recently found a poem which expresses this well.

> I painted a story. I used a pen.
> I changed it, rewrote it, again and again.
> I painted a picture. I searched for a word.
> That I hope would describe the sound that I heard.

I painted an image. I used my mind.
I rummaged around for the best word I can find.
I began with boom, but I've heard that before,
So I tried some new ones like crashing and more.

As many writers had used it when describing a sound,
I too searched the thesaurus, and guess what I found?
Thud, reverberation and crackle and growl,
Rumble and shudder and crackle and howl.

I painted a picture of the sound I have heard,
That rumbling, tumbling sound that occurred
As I lay in my bed cuddled up way down under
My soft downy quilt as I listened to the thunder.

TV ads

The loudness of the ads interrupting many TV programs is particularly annoying. This made the mute button my favorite button on the remote control. We turn our attention elsewhere until the program appears again. It is a small annoyance but enough of one to significantly reduce our focus on the program content.

Then I remembered that the legislature passed an act to limit the noise level of the ads to that of the associated program. For once, I thought, the legislators found an issue to which there would be no opposition.

I could not have been more wrong. The Mute Button Association objected violently. "They are trying to drive us out of business, cause more unemployment, and eventually ban us from the TV completely. We will form a union and then a political party to oppose this dastardly deed. We will call it the "**R**emote **U**nion **M**ute Button **P**arty," RUMP for short, for that is where the legislators will be sitting after we vote them out of office."

(Some suggested the party be called the "**F**ight **A**d **R**eform **T**oday," but the acronym deflects the purpose of our organization.)

The RUMP must have won the battle. The ads are still loud. We are thinking of forming and opposition party to roast the RUMP.

Writing a Creative Epic

I was going to do some writing. The day was clear of any commitments. How nice it will be to put all other worldly worries aside and focus on the challenge of letting my mind ramble through the fog until it finds a clear road ahead. It is 11:00 AM as I sit down at the computer after all personal chores of the day have been done. A blank sheet pops up on the monitor ready to record the epic creation. Blank is appropriate as it matches the immediate state of my mind. I stare at the monitor screen waiting to be overwhelmed by ideas.

The phone rings. Good thing that it rang before I was in the midst of translating my enthusiasm for a subject to paper. That would have deflated my inertia as though the balloon filled with ideas was suddenly popped. It was a friend of my wife's asking to talk to her. "She is at a medical appointment." I replied. "Take a message for her: Would she reschedule the book club meeting for tomorrow as I cannot host it as scheduled." she said. "Here are the other nine women who should be notified. Take them down." She demanded. "She may have their phone numbers. I can't contact them as I am already late for another appointment."

"If you will hold for just a second I will get pencil and paper so I can write down their names," I responded, trying to make my voice sound pleasant." Please hurry." came the urgent reply.

"OK, go ahead," I said. Just as she gave me the first name the last bit of lead fell out of the pencil. "I will need to have you wait just a second more as I try to find lead for the pencil."

Now where did I put the lead? Did this pencil take 0.5mm or 0.7 mm lead? The answer was nowhere to be found on the pencil. "Look," she announced impatiently, "I don't have time. The bridge group wants to start playing at 11:15 today and it almost that time already."

I resisted telling her what I was thinking. But she certainly provided great content for the creative piece I am going to write.

Words Scrambled in My Head

Sometimes I have a particular subject already in my mind when I sit down to write. Much of the time, however, I have to wait and think about a subject about which to write. Ideas leapfrog in my head. I stand motionless inside my head, reaching for something, but not nimble enough to grasp it.

The words start by too fast to connect. Were others to be able to look inside my brain, I'm sure they would think of me as being a mixed up guy, staring at the paper with my mouth agape because I can't begin to connect the words into a meaningful story.

My mind eventually intensely focuses on a topic when the phone suddenly rings.

"Hello Mr. Hanson. This is Mary at Dr. Jones office. We have your pre- registration information for your appointment next week. Missing, however, is the pharmacy to which any prescriptions should be sent. What is the name of the pharmacy?"

I respond with, "Ah, Ah, it's ah….," a long pause while my brain was trying to put Humpty Dumpty together again.

"Are you still there, Mr. Hanson?" the somewhat annoyed voice at the other end continued after a while.

"Yes I am. I'm just searching through my records to get the information." Now that should further raise the impression that I am not all there. Eventually I provided her with the information requested; glad to get back to writing before the idea evaporates.

"One more question," Mary responded. "What is your second-ary insurance company?" My mind now almost paralyzed, the question wrestled with my memory. I wish she had called just a few minutes before I attempted to do this creative writing. I could have answered the questions directly.

Another long wait for my response. I'm sure that this wait further embedded the idea that I am an idiot. I eventually provided the answer and hoped that Mary would not be the receptionist when I arrive at the doctor's office for my appointment.

By this time I had been doing such an exhaustive amount of thinking I was upset and tired. A nap should do the trick.

I'll start again tomorrow to unscramble the words hopefully still residing in my head.

THOUGHT PROVOKING

Admirable Qualities

The qualities which I admire in others are those by which I try to live. Some to share:

Integrity – I admire persons who keep their word, don't lie, adhere to a code of ethics, and adhere to principles of common decency; persons who have the courage to stand up for their own beliefs. Can one admire a person who goes behind one's back, badmouths others and spreads rumors and confidences?

Common sense – Have you ever met a person who has a very high IQ but no common sense? Education and intelligence are very desirable qualities. However the ability to solve a most puzzling problem and to be widely knowledgeable does not make one a great friend if social skills, the ability to listen and to relate to others are missing.

Sense of humor – Life with its many ups and downs is made much easier by having a sense of humor. Surrounding oneself with others who have one makes life much easier. How hard it would be to live with a person who has little or no sense of humor.

Self confidence – Everyone is low on confidence occasionally. A person with literally no self-esteem however is usually driven by self preservation; doing almost anything, lying, bad mouthing, and spreading confidences to feel important. No matter how much love and care is poured into them, it will all leak out of the sieve of low self esteem. It will never make them feel loved or good enough.

Kindness and Generosity – A kind and generous person will keep another's best interests in mind. This person knows how to put another's needs ahead of his own, when needed. He will find a way to avoid making recipients feel beholden or diminished.

Finding Serenity

Endless fields of grain swaying in a gently breeze; a clear stream splashing along rock imbedded channels guarded by beautiful green trees along its embankment; or majestic snow capped mountains reflected in calm blue lakes nestled at their feet, create havens of serenity.

Indeed these pastures of plenty penetrate our souls. They generate serenity and a deep feeling of pleasure and peace.

Yet pastures of plenty exist within each of us no matter how difficult one's life may seem at times. Itzhak Perlman, the violinist leaves us with just such an inspiration. Stricken with polio as a child, he has braces on both legs and walks with the aid of two crutches. At concerts he walks painfully but majestically on stage, sits down slowly, puts the crutches on the floor, undoes the clasps on his braces, reaches for his violin and nods to the conductor to begin.

At one concert something went wrong. After playing the first few bars one could clearly hear one of the strings on his violin break. All expected him to reverse the painful process to limp off the stage to obtain another violin. He did not. He waited a moment and then signaled the conductor to begin again. He played the entire symphony on three strings with such passion, power and purity as had never been heard before.

After a moment of silence, the audience rose to their feet, cheering to show their appreciation for what he had done. He smiled, wiped the sweat from his brow and in a quiet, pensive and reverent tone said, "You know, sometimes it is the artist's task to find out how much music you can still make with what you have left."

What a powerful line that was.

So, perhaps it is our task, in this shaky, fast-changing, bewildering world in which we live, is to find the music 'which exists within each of us.' When that is no longer possible we must find peace, pleasure and serenity with what we have left.

My Search for GOD

In 1956, our five year old daughter asked me a question at dinner which stunned me. "Daddy, if God made the earth, who made God?" My immediate reaction was to say, "Be quiet and eat your vegetables." But I held my tongue.

After some thought I knew that I must give her an answer which a five year old could understand. It took me a day or two to find an answer. I found it in two things which she knew, our puppy dog and the TV set.

"Susan, what if our TV set broke. Do you think that our puppy could fix it?" She laughed. "Of course the puppy cannot understand how to fix the TV set. That is just how we do not understand how God was made."

That seemed to satisfy her, but not me. I had lived through three years of fear and persecution before fleeing Germany and lost over 80 of my uncles, aunts and cousins who were killed in concentration camps during the Holocaust. I had learned of other massive genocides, massacres which had occurred over the ages and still occur today. How could a benevolent God permit such atrocities? Is there really such a God?

Of course there is. I only needed to look at the sky, to see the blooming of the earth, the very complexity of our own human bodies, how far humanity had developed since human like creatures first inhabited the earth. Some power well beyond our understanding guided and established the millions of suns and systems in the universe. It created the earth and a system to feed and sustain the millions of us and the creatures which populate the earth and the oceans.

My search over the subsequent years for a concept of God which I could accept, yet one which allowed for such atrocities to exist, occupied my more thoughtful moments. It was the technical education as an engineer which eventually led to a concept with which I could live. It generated optimism for the future, and it provided a guide for my daily living.

First let me explain viscous flow. It is a slow moving fluid in which all particles of the fluid flow parallel to the axis of a containing pipe with very little mixing occurring.

When the pipe is warmed from the outside, the particles of the fluid will not be at the same temperature across the internal diameter of the pipe. The water near the wall of the pipe would be warmer than it is at the center. Yet the overall temperature of the fluid will continue to rise as it flows along.

Visualize a pipe which starts at the beginning of time and ends at infinity, a time without end. Very cold water enters this pipe at the beginning. Heat surrounding the pipe warms the fluid as it slowly flows along the pipe. By the time the water nears infinity, it is almost as warm as the outside temperature which has influenced it, yet which it can never achieve.

Now, let us cut a slice across the pipe at any point as one would slice a sausage. We measure the temperature of the water over the exposed surface. Indeed, the temperature is not the same across this surface. It is warmer near the wall of the pipe and cooler near the center as little mixing of the fluid has occurred. Yet the overall temperature has indeed risen from that at its very cold beginning. The water cannot see through the walls of the pipe to see the source which is causing its temperature to rise. It can only feel it.

Let us then visualize that it is not a fluid but the slow march of the human race from the beginning of time. I believe we would agree that conditions for and relationships between us today are much better than existed, say, among cavemen (and their women.) Some force has driven this gradual improvement toward virtue and morality in personal relationships. Yet, human beings cannot see the force exerted on them through the walls of this "pipe" over the eons.

The slice we take across the pipe exposes conditions in our life time, a tiny period in the march of the human race from its beginning. The warmer spots (the people) have adopted more of the characteristics we attribute to God, how to relate to each other and how to relate to this power, each in our own way. The colder spots still revert to the same jungle mentality which existed since prehistoric times, when taking a life had no meaning or consequences.

Thus the horrible atrocities which still occur today, from Darfur, to Yugoslavia, in the Sudan, Serbs against Croatians, Iraq, Egypt, Syria killing its own people, to the murders which occur in our streets.

It is this external force which to me is God. We cannot see it through the walls of the pipe. We strive to describe it, but we do not know "who made God," the "warmth" which impacts humanity.

It is near infinity when all humanity finally reaches the temperature outside the pipe, the characteristics we attribute to God. We cannot become God just as there is no end to infinity. Human beings however can and have continued to adopt the attributes which we assign to God over the eons.

This long range view provided an affirmation that there is indeed a God. It is a cause for optimism. It is a guide for me to do all I can to help my children be better in their action and relationships than I may have been, to do what I can to improve the quality of life for others in the environment in which we live.

Yet this left me feeling that this concept still left a void. How can this unseen force, which impacts all humanity and causes constellations to form and disintegrate, the sun to provide us with light and warmth, also be a personal God? Where is this presence to provide the spiritual comfort I need? Whom do I thank for the many blessings and indeed miracles I have experienced? Who hears my prayers?

I recall my mother's last words as I was leaving for deployment abroad during World War II. "Whenever you feel that you are in danger repeat the words *God be with me* three times." As a macho 18 year old this struck me as mere wives tales. Yet when in particular danger during combat I did indeed utter these words. I realized then as I have since, we need a personal God also for many additional reasons.

This void troubled me for many years. Slowly an answer which eased this discomfort developed. Our subconscious is God's presence within us. It is the soul which was breathed into us by this awesome invisible force at birth. It is the depository of our prayers.

The soul grows with each experience and with each prayer of thanks we utter, with each act of kindness we perform. It alerts us when we are about to do the wrong thing, even though we may proceed to do so anyway. We have been given the free will to act. It eventually makes us rue the act and guides us not to repeat it. It makes us feel good when we have done something worthwhile.

It accepts our thanks for all of our blessings. It survives to return to its source when our body returns to the earth. It thus is my connection to the power we call God, the personal God who hears my thanks and my prayers.

This is a personal concept which satisfies my search for this magnificent, indescribable power which we call God. It may well not be the end of my search which my five year old daughter initiated so many years ago. It is the abode however in which I find the comfort to live and it guides my actions and decisions.

Our Choice

We cannot choose to be born into a family living in freedom in this great country of ours. We cannot choose the environment in which we are raised, slums, refugee camps, nice homes, clean neighborhood. We cannot choose our parents. Yet the quality of our upbringing and environment begins to shape our behavior.

Does this mean that we have no choice in life? Yes and no.

Certainly we had no choice in life during our baby years. We were totally dependent on our parents who made all the choices and decisions and assumed responsibilities for their choices. Then come the teen age years when we began to make choices, often based on youthful exuberance and lack of experience. We have growing freedom to make some of our own decisions but learn that our choices will have consequences.

Successful people at all levels, business and political leaders, artists, actors, philanthropists, volunteers, athletes etc. who have made and are making significant contributions to their communities and to our nation, have proven that their lives were not determined by the environment in which they were raised. It was determined by the forks along the road they chose to travel, absorbing the bumps along the way, that they achieved success. They had control of the car.

What power do they possess? The same power we have, the power to choose the life we want to live. We cannot change the past, nor control the curves or the bumps on the road which takes us through life. We can only make tomorrow better.

We can swear at the bumps and skid off the curves and damage the car. But it does not help the situation to blame our problems on those who have built the roads. It is within our power however to help improve the road for others and to enjoy the scenery along the way. That choice, for the balance of our lives, is ours and ours alone.

Quiet Dignity

What is "Quiet Dignity?" Can it be recognized when someone walks into a room? Is it a person's appearance, bearing, attire, attitude, or status in life? Can it be the laborer, who goes about his solitary work routine and comes home from a grueling day, who finds time to interact with his children? Is this "quiet dignity?"

Is it possible that quiet dignity is like a perfume? Those who emanate it are scarcely aware of it? Is it a sign of ardor or lack of strength?

My thoughts turn to some of the experiences we had while living in England. We became acutely aware of the deep class distinctions which still existed there. Royalty generally, the Lords, Earls, Dukes, Princesses, Duchesses, Viscounts, their families and descendents, considered those of non-royal blood inferior and looked down on them. Yet, when they entered the room they exuded an air of dignity, despite the fact that so many of them had become so impoverished that they rented out a part of the castles in which they lived to 'commoners' in order to survive. Should 'Quiet Dignity' be assigned to them? Is there a distinction between quiet dignity, pretentiousness and superiority?

This class distinction went beyond those of royal blood. It extended also to those 'commoners' whose ancestors were born in England.

I recall sitting in a restaurant at Heathrow airport with Hugh, a quite dignified and successful headhunter I had hired to search for a plant manager for our Belgium plant. A flight crew which had just flown a South African Airways 707 to London entered the restaurant.

Hugh turned to me and said, "I wouldn't fly with those buggers for all the money in the world."

"Why not?" I asked.

"Because they are hardly out of the bush" he answered. This attitude by middle and upper class British toward former colonists was not uncommon.

Is 'quiet dignity' a characteristic one senses internally or is it one which others recognize?

Slowly a poem, *The Person in the Glass*, (Author Unkown) comes to mind.

THE PERSON IN THE GLASS

When you get what you want in the struggle for self
And the world makes you king for the day,
Then go to the mirror and look at yourself
And see what that person has to say.

For it isn't your father, or mother, or spouse,
Whose judgment you must pass.
The person whose verdict counts most in life
Is the person staring back from the glass.

That person is the one to please, never all the rest,
It's that person who is with you clear to the end,
And you've passed the most dangerous, difficult test
If the person in the glass is your friend.

You may be like Jack Horner and 'chisel' a plum
And think you're a wonderful guy
But the person in the glass says you're only a bum
If you can't look that person straight in the eye.

You can fool the whole world down the pathway of years
And get pats on the back as you pass,
But your final reward will be heartache and tears
If you've cheated that person in the glass.

It leads me to the belief that 'Quiet Dignity' is something which we feel within, when our actions lead us to like the person in the glass.

Serendipity

The accident of finding something good or useful, while not specifically searching for it. In other words, luck.

A debate has been raging for many ages whether one would rather have luck or an education. Each side of the debate makes very good points to support their opinion.

You find something you were not looking for and it changes the world. After the discovery one wonders why it took so long to arrive at something so obvious. Was it luck or was it education which led one there?

Many discoveries which were accidents, for example:

Charles Goodyear had been obsessed with finding a way to make a rubber useful. When he accidentally dropped a piece of rubber mixed with sulfur onto a hot stove, he discovered the vulcanization process for rubber. We all ride on his accidental discovery today. George deMestral was curious why some burrs stuck so tightly to his clothing. He had no intention of inventing a fastener (Velcro).

The discoverer of the laser, Charles Townes, was teased by his colleagues about the irrelevance of his discovery. Today the applications and the beneficial effects of the laser in the world around us abound. Compact discs, eyesight correction, microsurgery, data storage and retrieval, are other examples of products used throughout the world which were initially thought to be irrelevant.

A lab technician was doing experiments to develop a replacement for leather. After many experiments she spilled some of the liquid on her tennis shoes. She complained to her supervisor that she was unable to wash the shoes. Water would not penetrate the coating. She wanted the company to replace them. That led to the discovery of Scotch Guard.

I would argue that the inventor of these and other discoveries, penicillin, x-rays, Teflon, dynamite, etc., had to be educated to pursue a worthwhile object. It was a lucky accident, which led them to discover something widely beneficial. We can pursue an education and acquire knowledge, but we cannot teach alertness and the acquisition of luck. I would choose the education. Only then can serendipity, luck, follow.

I'll Just Be Me

Strong opposing opinions about how we should or should not make decisions, act, prioritize our tasks, handle controversy, articulate a written communication, etc., are often expressed by others not familiar with the conditions which prompt our action. If we try to accommodate them all, the outcome can be catastrophic. Knowledgeable advice is of course very desirable.

I am reminded of a man, woman and child who set out on a pilgrimage from Jerusalem to Bethlehem with their donkey about 1500 years ago. The man, riddled by arthritis, rode on the donkey as they departed.

They were not very far down the road when one of the pilgrims coming the other way shouted, "How can you, a strong man, ride while your poor wife has to walk? You ought to be ashamed of yourself." He got down and helped his wife get on the donkey.

Shortly thereafter they encountered another pilgrim. Angrily he shouted at the wife, "How can you ride the donkey while your little child who has to take so many more steps than you has to walk?" She got down and helped the child mount the donkey.

They still had a long way to go when another peasant shaking his head yelled, "How can you, the head of the house walk while your child rides? What's this country coming to?"

When they arrived in Bethlehem all three were carrying the donkey.

Good or bad in the eyes of others, I'll just be me. It is I who will be bearing the responsibility for the outcome.

Sometimes I Wonder

Having observed some rather rancorous election campaigns makes me wonder; is degrading the character of political opponents is the only way to get elected to political office? Do the politicians understand that a possible effect is that a significant portion of electorate feels that only crooks and immoral people run for office? Does this contribute to a loss of faith in our government?; to the growing ground swell to 'throw the bums out?' Does this contribute to low voter turnout?

Very qualified, experienced, committed, intelligent and pragmatic leaders do serve in our government. How did they ever achieve these high positions? Was it before character assassination became the vogue?

Candidates make many promises to get elected, promises which they cannot deliver. They suffer from information overload once in office and become aware of the conditions of which they were not aware, or which they chose to ignore during their campaign.

Sometimes I wonder if qualified candidates could get elected were they to have the following platform:

1. State clearly what the issues are and what their objectives are on each issue.

2. State that they may not have all of the information to which they will have access once in office. This information may cause them to compromise on some the issues. They will however work to achieve the best results possible to reach their announced objectives.

3. Point out the flaws in the positions of opposing candidates but will stick to the issues without personal attacks.

I wonder, would a significant portion of the electorate vote for them?

What is the 'IT?'

As again this Seder we together sit,
I begin to ponder, are we losing it?
What is the 'IT'' which causes concern?
What is it that's so important to learn?

Why bring it up at our Seder tonight?
We read from a book and that's alright.
When I was a child that's how it was done.
I just had to sit there but that was no fun.

Every word from the Hagaddah was loudly read.
It was well after midnight before I got to bed.
I understood not one word of the Hebrew text.
My mind was focused on the meal which comes next.

Then as I grew older I began to see
What observance of the holidays has done for me.
The world is imperfect because people are.
We are given free will which some carry too far.

When winds of change thus blow in my face,
What spiritual strengths do I have to embrace?
Can I possibly overcome the awful distress,
And not succumb to a depressing morass?

When the winds are kind we may stop to ask;
Why am I here, what is my life's task?
What guide should I follow when I exercise my will?
What mission on this earth was I sent to fulfill?

Each observance we follow, such as the Seder tonight,
Brings hope and strength to which I hold tight.
What is the 'IT" from the Passover meal
Which presents to us such an important appeal?

Within each soul there is an unrelenting yearning
For dignity and freedom which require our earning.
There are guidelines we must follow, we must show restraint
Lest the freedom of others we tend to constrain.

The road from oppression to freedom wasn't easy.
Many fleeing from Egypt felt panic and uneasy.
Hardships and problems caused many to question,
Would it not be better to return to oppression?

Among deeper meanings which the Exodus present,
Is that each life will experience some significant torment.
That belief in a power much greater than we
Will from such harsh ordeal surely set us free.

There are rules and guidelines which freedom imply.
The Constitution and the Torah are ones we go by.
Each holiday will provide us anew
A deeper 'IT' to see tough times through.

There is another component to the Seder 'It'
Which for this observance is a particular fit.
It's the only holiday we celebrate at home.
It's the family gathering to instill further Sholom.

A special gift I never realized I was missing
Is the value of the Seder, I sat quietly reminiscing.

It's an 'IT' which Savta brought into our marriage.
It's an important one that we must not disparage.

Savta provides the glue to hold family together.
A haven and warmth in wonderful weather.
A port in the storm when the headwinds winds blow
A source of support to help ease our woe.

Mobility and opportunity are one threat to IT
Causing family to distant places to split.
Deeper holiday values become more distant,
To life's headwinds we can become less resistant.

So let us celebrate the IT at our Seder tonight
As a family we gather to warmly unite.

Two Crows

Enjoying the scene out of our window one sunny afternoon, I saw two crows feeding in our yard. I expected a noisy flock to join them but they never did. Only two crows appeared the following day, again unaccompanied by a flock. My curiosity led me to learn more about crows. I found that these very intelligent birds mate for life and that their offsprings stay with the parents for some time after being born. That led me to write the following story:

Two intelligent crows, Casper and Cassy, had been flying with a flock of hundreds for over a year. Casper had become enchanted with Cassy and felt the need to get to know her better. Fighting off contending suitors had gotten to Casper and the continuous and loud cawing of the flock had prevented a more intimate conversation with Cassy.

"Let's blow this crowd and venture out by ourselves for awhile." said Casper.

"How can I?" Cassy responded. "I have many friends here and I will miss them. Not only that, but I know the lawns, parking lots, and garbage dumps we all visit and would hate to start looking for new ones again."

"But you have also heard people plot to get rid of us 'pests'; chasing us away, planting decoy owls to scare us, and shooting at us. I will always recognize the guy who shot me. He must still be around here. If I ever find him, I'll buzz him and yell at him and smack him on the head until I drive him nuts." replied Casper trying his best to convince her.

"I like you a lot." said Cassy. "But where will we find other places for food and a friendlier atmosphere?"

"I know of just such a place. I have a friend there. If you like it and we can establish ourselves there."

"You are very persuasive, Casper."

So they took off in their unique flight style, methodically flapping their broad, rounded wings with tips like fingers, rarely broken up with glides.

Enroute they stopped at a grassy lawn to enjoy the seeds remaining on the ground and to rest.

"Tell me about the friend to whom we are headed." Cassy asked at one of the stops.

"I was injured while quite young. My parents had been killed and I did not know what to do. A young human found me in the yard and took me to a wildlife rehabilitation center which housed other crows and blue jays. This human took care of me, fed me and nursed me back to good health. I would chatter at him which surprised him. I looked forward to his coming into the room at nine in the morning. I would jump to a perch and start chatting. When he worked at night, I would swoop down and sit on his shoulder. I was so grateful for his help."

"You mean that there actually are humans who care for us and not look as us as pests?" Cassy asked. "We are crows living our own lives and feeding our families."

"Yes there are. After I was released to join a flock I would often return to see him. He would wave to me and feed me peanuts. That is unusual for a human being as they rarely distinguish us, one from another."

Cassy and Casper agreed to marry and stay near the rehabilitation center.

Eventually Cassy became very restless being away from the friends in the flock. Even Casper saw that this was not a natural way for them to live.

They returned to the old flock where they raised a family and where Casper found and took great delight bombing the man who shot him.

About the Author

Fred S. Hirsekorn was born in Germany in 1924. Almost 12 years old, he, his parents and grandmother fled Germany in 1936 and immigrated to the US. He attended grade and high school in Kansas City, Missouri and entered the military service in 1942. Armored force basic training at Camp Campbell, Kentucky was followed by six months in the Army Special Training Program at Ohio State University. He was sent to Camp Campbell to join the 14th Armored Division heading for combat in Europe when the ASTP program was abruptly closed. He rose to the rank of first sergeant.

After graduating from the University of Kansas with an MS, Ch.E. degree his jobs took him to New Martinsville, West Virginia, then to Wichita, Kansas, and in 1965, to St. Paul, Minnesota. His various assignments at Economics Laboratory, from where he retired in 1986, included service as Vice President, European Operations. He then established his consulting company, GMS, Inc., from where he retired in 1994.

Hirsekorn held leadership positions in the American Red Cross, Boy Scouts, Minnesota Diversified Industries, and the Minnesota Governor's Commission on Employment of Handicapped Persons.

He and his wife live in Lilydale, Minnesota.

CPSIA information can be obtained at www.ICGtesting.com
Printed in the USA
LVOW11s0409110814

398514LV00001B/3/P